MEDITATIO
BEGINN~~~

*THINK AND ACT LIKE A ZEN MONK WITH THE POWEROF
MINDFULNESS AND VISUALIZATION AND STOP BEING
ANXIOUS AND STRESSED FORNOTHING*

MASTER GUIDED AND SLEEP MEDITATION

JAY LUCADO

Published by
Jason Thawne Publishing House
© Jay Lucado
Meditation For Beginners: Think and Act Like A Zen
Monk With The Power of Mindfulness and Visualization
and Stop Being Anxious and Stressed For Nothing
(Master Guided and Sleep Meditation)

ISBN 978-1-9992979-0-9

This document is geared towards providing exact and reliable information in regards to the topic and issue covered. The publication is sold with the idea that the publisher isn't required to render accounting, officially permitted, or otherwise, qualified services. If advice is necessary, legal or even professional, a practiced individual in the profession should be ordered.

- From a Declaration of Principles which was accepted and approved equally by a Committee of the American Bar Association and a Committee of Publishers and Associations.

The information provided herein is stated to be truthful and consistent, in that any liability, in terms of inattention or otherwise, by any usage or abuse of any policies, processes, or directions contained within is the solitary and also utter responsibility of the recipient reader. Under no circumstances will any legal responsibility or blame be held against the publisher for any reparation, damages, or

CHAPTER 1: DIFFERENT METHODS AND PRACTICES OF MEDITATION 1

CHAPTER 2: MEDITATION AND YOUR HEALTH.................. 9

CHAPTER 3: MEDITATING FOR MY FIRST TIME 23

CHAPTER 4: PREPARING FOR MEDITATION 28

CHAPTER 5: MEDITATION.. 35

CHAPTER 6: TYPES OF MEDITATION 42

CHAPTER 7: EMOTIONAL MEDITATION 61

CHAPTER 8: BEYOND PROBIOTICS: HOW MEDITATION HEALS THE GUT 65

CHAPTER 9: WHAT IS THE MANTRA, AND WHY IS IT NEEDED? 87

CHAPTER 10: PEOPLE VERY RARELY HAVE THE TIME TO SIT STILL ANYMORE 92

CHAPTER 11: MEDITATION TECHNIQUES FOR INNER PEACE 103

CHAPTER 12: THE ART OF VISUALIZATION..................... 112

CHAPTER 13: MEDITATION: STEP BY STEP GUIDE 117

CHAPTER 14: YOU ARE ALREADY "MEDITATING"?........ 122

CHAPTER 15: THE MEDITATION PROCESS....................... 125

CHAPTER 16: COLOR IMAGINATION HEALING 130

CHAPTER 17: SIGNS THAT A PERSON IS OVERLOADED BY STRESS.. 133

CHAPTER 18: REFLECTION TO CAUSE REST 136

CHAPTER 19: MEDITATION IN YOUR DAILY TASKS......... 142

CHAPTER 20: FORGIVENESS... 147

CHAPTER 21: HOW TO SKYROCKET YOUR CREATIVITY WITH MEDITATION 151

CHAPTER 22: USING MEDITATION FOR GOALS 155

Chapter 1: Different Methods And

Practices Of Meditation

There are numerous methods of meditation out there and everybody finds their own way through this path. Some forms work much better for some people than others. You may have to try a few different methods before you find the one that's right for you, or you may even find more than one that you enjoy and go back and forth between them. This is alright too. One suggestion that you'll find in most meditation lessons is to stick to one at a time until you learn enough about a particular style to switch, don't overwhelm yourself with unreasonable expectations. You will not become a meditation master overnight. When trying a new method don't just give up right away because you think it's not working. Give each method at least a week before trying a new one. By doing this you will be able to reap the benefits from each style before actually trying another one. Remember: patience is key.

Mindfulness

The most widely known and practiced form of meditation is known as Mindfulness Meditation. This particular method combines concentration with awareness, and is synonymous with the Theravada Buddhist practice of "insight meditation" or vipassana (A Pali word). Usually the practitioner of this practice will concentrate on something for long periods of time such as their breath, thoughts, sounds, or other bodily feelings. Keep in mind that mindfulness does not mean you have to quiet your mind. Mindfulness is the natural ability to observe your mind without responding to it.

One type of Mindfulness meditation is called "Zen" meditation. In Zen meditation there is more focus on the posture that the person is sitting in. You want to sit comfortably with your back straight. With mindfulness meditation you want to be sure to notice all thoughts that arise, as

2

they arise. While doing this, you don't want to dwell on your thoughts, but simply notice them and allow them to pass on their own. The goal of this meditation is to become the silent observer. The key is to realize that you are not your thoughts and that you, as the observer, are the one noticing these thoughts. This method of meditation is said to lead to deeper understanding of the Self and what our place in the universe is.

Loving Kindness

Loving Kindness meditation is also known as Metta Bhavana, and the purpose of this meditation is to develop a stronger sense of compassion towards self and other living beings. This meditation includes a combination of breathing exercises and positive affirmations. You would say things such as: May I be happy, may I be healthy, may I be free from suffering. After intending positive things toward yourself, you then wish these things upon others. As you move outwards with this you eventually start to hope for positivity among all beings.

3

Studies have shown (on pubmed.gov) that loving kindness meditation helps with migraines, chronic pain, PTSD, and schizophrenia symptoms. This particular form of meditation is very good for gaining a stronger sense of connection with yourself and the world around you.

Mantra

In mantra meditation the practitioner decides upon a specific mantra (such as "OM") and repeats this mantra each time they exhale. After doing this for as long as it feels comfortable the person may decide to either continue chanting or finish in silence. Either way is fine. Just like any other forms of meditation, the amount of time you do it is up to you. Many people have heard the term "OM" but may not know what it means. The term "OM" is actually Sanskrit in origin and it is said that every sound or syllable can be found in this particular chant. This is said because when you pronounce "OM" you actually pronounce it more like "AUM". When pronounced correctly the throat makes the "A" sound, the "U" represents the

4

speech itself moving forward from your throat through your lips, and the "M" is the closing of the sound. In this way the term "OM" is created through all parts of the mouth.

"OM" or "AUM" also represents the three periods of Time. The "A" sound represents the beginning of time, the "U" sound represents the preservation of time, and the "M" sound (you probably guessed it) represents the end of time. Even the symbol for this sound has symbolic import correlating with the symbolism for the sounds themselves.

Guided

In guided meditation you meditate while listening to an audio that guides you through different sensations and mental states. Usually recorded audios for guided meditation include verbal guidance combined with soft relaxing music or sounds. There are many different types of guided meditations with many different purposes, each one as valid as the next. Remember: do not get too caught up on whether a meditation is "wrong" or "right". The only wrong meditation is no meditation.

One cool thing about this form of meditation is that it takes your focus off of yourself and puts it on the person's message being used to guide you. Now this isn't for everybody as some people prefer to do it themselves. It is fine to use guided meditation though, as you can look at it as a way to ask for guidance when you are first starting out with developing your own personal practice. It's still you doing the meditation.

Yoga

You may be wondering what yoga has to do with meditation. Well what most people don't know is that yoga is a form of meditation. People that practice yoga consider it "meditation in action". In yoga, focusing on your breath is also a crucial part of the process. Yoga is not designed for exercise like most people in the West believe. It originated as a spiritual discipline. Yoga actually translates to "union" and refers to the union of lower Self with higher Self. Although it's not exactly designed for exercise, you will also get many physical benefits from doing yoga. This of course would require more research and study as yoga is its own practice all together.

Transcendental

Transcendental meditation is a form of meditation that was promoted by a man named Maharishi Mahesh in the 20th century. This particular branch of meditation is meant to be taught specifically by a trained teacher. And certain classes need to be taken in order to learn the methods for this particular type of meditation which cost a good amount of money. There is much criticism with this method, but you must do your own research in order to figure out if this is the route that you want to take.

These are only a few of the methods that are out there and if you don't find that one of these work adequately for you, then continue researching other methods.

If you're seriously determined to learn meditation, then you will find one that suits you better.

Chapter 2: Meditation And Your Health

- STRESS

Stress is a common issue in the society today. It results in different forms of health issues and poses a threat to our general wellbeing. Researchers believe that the common epidemics of hypertension and heart disease are due to stress. Most individuals frequently came across a sudden stress or threat in their activities and our bodies respond with a 'fight or flight' response. This response is absolutely normal but the issue is that the individual goes through a sort of 'adrenaline rush' due to the release of the epinephrine and norepinephrine hormones. These hormones, in turn, bring about an increase in blood pressure and pulse rate. They also cause blood to flow faster to the muscles and make breathing quite faster than normal. Therein lies the problem of the 'fight or flight' response.

Research has shown however that meditation can help to counter the effect which the response would have on our bodies. The form of meditation recommended is the relaxation technique and practicing it results in a state of deep relaxation wherein our breathing, pulse rate, level of blood pressure level and metabolism are reduced. When we teach our bodies to attain this level of relaxation on a daily basis, our mood is enhanced, blood pressure level is lowered, digestion is improved and amount of stress which we go through is generally decreased.

This relaxation technique is done by sitting quietly with a good posture and eyes closed. A word, sound or phrase is then repeated silently for about ten to twenty minutes. The word, sound or phrase to be used could likely be one which conveys a special or deep meaning to you. A sitting posture is also recommended during meditation in order to avoid falling asleep. Slowly begin to relax your muscles from your feet and then move up to your face. Your breathing should be in a natural way and through your nose not the mouth. During a meditation session, thoughts or worries which could intrude and disturb the session should be ignored by placing all your focus on the word, phrase or sound you are uttering depending on your choice. To achieve maximum results, meditation should be done in a place that is quiet and has no distractions.

• INCREASED IMMUNITY

The relaxation technique of meditation has also been proven to boost immunity in patients of cancer who are at the recovery stage. The Ohio state university, after conducting a series of studies has shown that when breast cancer patients practiced progressive muscular relaxation on a daily basis, the risk of a recurrence is greatly reduced. Another study conducted at the same university also showed that carrying out relaxation exercises for about a month can boost the natural killer cells in elderly people thereby giving them the ability to resist tumors and viruses greatly too.

• HIGH LEVEL OF FERTILITY

Various universities in different parts of the world have proven that meditation helps to increase the level of fertility in humans. The University of Western Australia has conducted studies which prove that at a time when relaxed, it is much more probable that women will conceive as opposed to when they are stressed. The researches of Trakya University in Turkey too have found out that, with the elimination of stress, sperm count and motility is reduced. This study makes the suggestion that meditation can also serve as a boost of male fertility.

• REDUCED BLOOD PRESSURE LEVEL

According to a study carried out at the Harvard Medical School, the practice of meditation is able to reduce the pressure of blood. This is done by making the body not as responsive as usual to the stress hormones; it carries out the same work as any medication whose work is to reduce blood pressure. A British medical journal report also found out that patients who have learned and mastered how to relax have a significantly lower blood pressure in comparison to those who have not.

- CALMNESS

There is a clear distinction between people who meditate and people who do not. The obvious difference is that for a meditative person, a particular thought in question occurs but is witnessed by the mind only; for a person who does not practice meditation however, the thought occurs and dominates the person's mind and body. In summary, both minds go through upsetting thoughts but it is seen as just another by the meditative mind and is allowed to blossom and die as such. In the ordinary mind however, that disturbing thought brings about a 'storm' which starts to 'rage' continually and eventually leads to various issues. An individual who practices meditation is calmer in comparison to an individual who does not.

- ANTI-INFLAMMATION

When the body undergoes stress, it leads to inflammation and this has been linked to various diseases like arthritis, asthma and heart disease. Skin diseases like psoriasis have also been shown to be linked to inflammation by researchers of the Emory University in the US. By shutting off the normal response which the body is supposed to have towards stress, relaxation has the ability to prevent and also treat symptoms of inflammation. Through this, a study conducted by the McGill University of Canada has shown that the act of meditating improves symptoms or signs of the psoriasis skin condition clinically.

• SERVES AS A CURE FOR IRRITABLE BOWEL SYNDROME

Certain individuals suffer from the Irritable Bowel Syndrome. If they practice relaxation meditation twice in a day, symptoms of the syndrome such as diarrhea, bloating and constipation show a significant level of improvement. This type of meditation proved to be very effective for treating this Irritable Bowel Syndrome to the extent that the State University of New York recommends it for patients of the syndrome.

• PROVIDES EMOTIONAL BALANCE

14

By emotional balance, we mean being free from all sorts of neurotic behavior which is present due to a tortured or even traumatized self-esteem. Unhealthy emotional states and neurosis such as this can be addressed through the act of meditation, although quite difficult to be fully cured. When individuals begin to clear their consciousness of such emotional memories, the person in question begins to experience great emotional balance and a lot of emotional freedom also. This happens because the individual becomes more rational and is able to make decisions that are appropriate and true since the responses he or she will provide to certain matters are not given or determined by the emotional burdens which he or she is carrying.

• IMPROVES LEVEL OF GREY MATTER CONCENTRATION PRESENT IN THE BRAIN

An experiment was recently carried out by a group of some Harvard neuroscientists. This experiment involved some sixteen people who were put through a mindfulness course while making use of mindfulness in their daily activities and guided meditations for a period of eight weeks. After this period of time had lapsed, MRI scans showed that the level of concentration of grey matter present in parts of the brain which are involved in regulating emotions, sense of self, learning, memory etc. increased.

These were the results of just a short-term experiment. Studies have shown that people who meditate on a regular basis for long time display larger frontal volumes of grey matter.

• INCREASES THE ABILITY TO FOCUS EVEN WHEN DISTRACTIONS ARE PRESENT

It has been recorded that people with a greater experience of meditation show a higher level of connectivity in the brain networks that are in charge of controlling attention.

Neural relationships like this could be concerned with developing cognitive skills like getting detached from distractions and remaining focused.

• HELPS YOU TO PREPARE HOW TO DEAL WITH EVENTS THAT ARE STRESSFUL

The All India Institute of Medical Sciences records a study in which 32 adults who had never practiced the act of meditating before were used. This study showed proof that if individuals are able to practice meditation before a stressful event, the adverse effects which stress would normally have on them is reduced.

More than 20 different control studies taken from articles out of the PubMed, Cochrane Databases and PsycInfo magazines have shown that meditative prayers, meditation techniques, relaxation response and Yoga help in treating Premenstrual Syndrome (PMS) and some menopausal symptoms.

• BRINGS ABOUT A REDUCTION IN THE RISK OF PREMATURE DEATH AND ALZHEIMER'S

A research conducted recently which was published online in the Brain, Behavior and Immunity journal shows that meditating for only a period of 30 minutes daily does not only reduce the sense of loneliness but also lessens the risk of Alzheimer's, premature death, depression and the likes.

- MAY INCREASE YOUR LIFESPAN

The way by which our cells age are affected by Telomeres which are a vital part of our human cells. Some data have been found suggesting that there are some specific types of meditation which may have salutary effects on the length of telomeres and this is done by reducing the amount of cognitive stress and also by heightening the level of positive states of mind and hormonal factors which might be able to maintain telomeres in a better way.

- CAN HELP WITH ALCOHOL AND SUBSTANCE ADDICTION

18

Due to the effects it has on the areas linked with self-control in the brain, meditation can be quite useful to people who have addictions to certain things. In the case of smoking, this could likely be because practicing meditation assists people in separating their craving from the actual act of smoking. Therefore, craving does not always have to lead to smoking. Other studies have also proven that mindfulness-based relapse prevention (MBRP) and mindfulness-based cognitive therapy (MBCT) can also be very useful in treating some other types of addiction. Some other benefits which meditation provides are that-

• It reduces the level of blood lactate present in an individual's body. This, in turn, brings about a reduction in the amount of anxiety attacks he or she goes through.

• It brings about a reduction in pain related to tension. Such pains include tension headaches, muscle problems, joint problems, insomnia, and ulcers among others.

- It makes an individual have more energy. This is because you develop an inner source of energy in addition to the normal source.

- The production of serotonin is increased. This high level of production then brings about an improvement in an individual's behavior and mood.

- It increases a meditative individual's level of happiness.

- It brings about a development in a person's intuition. The mind is made sharper because relaxation helps an individual to gain focus and to expand through relaxation.

- It reduces atherosclerosis.

- An individual gains clarity on a lot of issues and also begins to have peace of mind or an increased level of peace of mind.

- It lowers the level of thickening of coronary arteries.

For students, teachers and staff too, meditation boosts their confidence and also provides more clarity and focus. They are able to get greater mental strength and become more dynamic and get gain more energy. Meditation is also proven to bring about a reduction in signs of depression and also hostility towards their colleagues. Their anxiety, somatic stress and reactivity levels are also lessened while they get an increase in their cognitive retention, positive emotions and general feelings of wellbeing and happiness. There was also an improvement in their sleeping patterns, academic performance, social skills and self-awareness.

On a spiritual ground also, meditation can help you to truly transform personally. Through the practice, you are able to have a deeper understanding and greater knowledge of yourself and this will naturally result into a greater level of self-discovery. The effortless or easy transition with which meditation is carried out helps you to easily become one with the infinite and also to see yourself as something or someone which cannot be detached or removed from the whole cosmos itself.

When a person gets into a meditative state, he or she comes into a space of calmness, vastness and joy. He or she then begins to transmit this into the environment thus bringing about harmony to the planet or creation.

To cap it all up, science has been able to confirm that meditating will help you to be healthier, make you happier, prevent you from getting various diseases and will also help you have a better performance in any mental or physical task you might want to carry out.

Written above are just some of the benefits that practices of meditation you can enjoy. Now that we have come to know how useful meditation is, it is time we discussed some of the various forms or types that exist, their origins and how they can be carried out especially by people who are just about to get in on some of the action.

Chapter 3: Meditating For My First Time

I wanted more than this beautiful story of letting go. I wanted the cure. One day, I grabbed the phone book and looked up meditation and I found The Zen Group. I rang them about meditation classes and I was invited to join them for weekly meditation.When I turned up the following week many of them were dressed in monks robes and I felt a little intimidated to say the least.

These people were very welcoming and compassionate towards me and I felt good. I knew that I'd come to the right place and people. This was an absolute life changing event for me.

The technique I was taught was counting my breath in for six counts and then counting the breath out for six counts. This was done continuously for one hour. It seem to take a lifetime. I would lose my count and then have to start back at one. This happened a lot during the hour but I felt relaxed and calm. Why do we lose count? We lose count because we are thinking. For example... We start counting the breath in one, two, three " oh what am i going to do when i get home?" You've just lost count by thinking about the future. What to do? Simply start back at one then two, three, four etc.

When it was time to finish we all simply said goodbye and that was it until the following week. I went home and continued to do my meditation each day and I finally had to see my psychiatrist. I thought that he was a bit nuts, so I decided it was time for me to finish treatment. I told him that I'd poured his meds down the sink and that I didn't need to come back. He sat back in his chair and said this " so what makes you think that you don't need treatment anymore? ". I said " because you can't help me as the answer is inside me and I will find it through Zazen meditation. " All he said was that I was correct.

I was amazed at his response, he didn't put up a fight or anything. He probably put me in the too hard basket. I don't presume that he cared about me, it was a job and he never seem to be present anyway. To care about me means that he would have compassion. We need to have awareness on the inside to have compassion on the outside. Compassion is an immensely beautiful quality to have as a human. To me, that's being a true human being. A psychiatrist is trying to adjust people back to what society considers is normal but society isn't normal and is in fact sick.

I am so grateful to have found meditation and to have become conscious as a by product. To be conscious is to be awake and taking responsibility for our thoughts and actions. When you're a conscious person you don't go around hurting others or stealing from people. Hurting and stealing from others is a lack of compassion.

Meditation has totally transformed my life and it will transform yours as well. People will notice the positive changes in you as you're becoming compassionate towards yourself and others.

Living in an unconscious way is living in a negative way, full of self importance, lack of empathy, hurting others, negativity, being deceitful, violent and so on. To me, living in an unconscious way is to suffer and have no freedom. In other words, to live unconsciously is to be reactive to every situation without ever considering the consequences of one's actions.

We never really arrive it's more of a moving towards being whole. For example, we move towards full consciousness and away from unconsciousness. We move towards enlightenment and away from ignorance. As we're moving towards being whole our quality of life is constantly improving. Also, we affect others in a positive way and create a domino effect. You're friends and family will notice the positive changes in you and may ask you what's going on. This is a great time to tell them about meditation and it's wonderful benefits that you're experiencing.

I remember when I first started meditating that I wasn't sure whether I was doing it correctly or not. When I started feeling its benefits I knew that I was doing something correct. Life just kept getting better and better, it still does. I can't imagine my life without meditation or what type of person I would be now if I hadn't begun to meditate.

I think that people don't meditate for various reasons and unfortunately they are totally unaware of what they're missing. It's like the saying that you don't know what you don't know. We're heavily conditioned by society to make fun of what we don't understand and to crucify people. Gee whiz, didn't we cop this at school as we weren't encouraged to think for ourselves. Why weren't we taught to meditate at school? What a huge missed opportunity for society. We need to observe everything deeply, to inquire, to question and to look at things intelligently. This is what a conscious person does naturally.

Chapter 4: Preparing For Meditation

By examining the meditation poses it is easy to see that they all have one thing in common. This being that they are all crafted around sitting on a broad base that appears to be deep rooted into the earth. If you sit up straight your body will act as a link between heaven and earth, and as so connects your physical existence with the spiritual dimension of being. As well as this spiritual aspect it could be considered that sitting up straight provides practical benefits also.

When you open your spine you are opening the channels that run through the center of your body and sitting upright encourages the circulation of energy which awakens your body on all levels, the mental, spiritual and physical. Sitting up straight is also the most comfortable to sit for prolonged periods and this is how you can be in tune with nature.

Many think that they could lean against a wall or object to have this type of straightness, however your body will tend to slouch one way or another and the point of meditation is to rely on your direct existence rather than relying on something supporting you.

Take up your position

We understand that trees need deep roots to prevent them from falling over as they grow and in the same way you need to find a comfortable position for your lower body which you can sustain for at least 15 minutes. There are a number of traditional postures that seem to work particularly well and although they are very different they all have one thing in common, this is that the pelvis tilts slightly forward which accentuates the natural curve of the lower back.

The following poses are the most traditional when meditating and are shown in order of difficulty, beginning with the easiest, although this is dependent on your particular body and degree of flexibility:

1.   Sitting in a chair

When choosing to sit in a chair to meditate the secret is to position your buttocks higher than your knees as this will tilt the pelvis forward and keep your back straight. Experiment using a cushion under your bottom, most importantly do not slouch.

2.   Kneeling

Kneeling can be hard on your knees if you do not have proper support. To maintain the correct position try positioning a cushion under your buttocks and between your feet this will also prevent these parts of your body falling asleep!

3.   Easy position

This position is not ideal for extended periods of sitting as it is not particularly stable and provides no back support. Sit on a cushion with your legs crossed in front of you, while your knees do not need to touch the floor, but you need to keep your back as straight as possible. This position can be stabilized by using a cushion under your knees and gradually decrease the height as your hips become more flexible.

When you are more au fait with these positions and can perform them for prolonged periods you can move onto the more difficult:

4.   Burmese Position

This is a pose that is synonymous and used throughout the south eastern areas of Asia. The pose involves putting both calves and legs on the floor in front of each other. This is quite an easy pose for beginners to master.

5.   Half Lotus

Whilst sitting on a cushion place one foot on the opposite thigh making sure that both knees are touching the floor to remain stable and prevent the spine from tilting to one side.

6.   Quarter Lotus

Similar to the half lotus apart from the foot rests on the calf of your opposite leg rather than the thigh.

7.   Full Lotus

With your buttocks supported by a cushion cross the left foot over the right thigh and vice versa.

The full lotus has been practiced all over the world for years, and whilst the most stable of poses this should not be attempted unless you are particularly flexible and you should always carry out some stretches prior to taking up this position.

Mediation is a practice that can help you to relieve the stresses and strains that are brought on by modern day. All you need is a quiet space and the ability to focus your attention plus a simple meditation technique. Armed with this, give it a go you really cannot go wrong.

How to Prepare for Meditation

Meditation is simple and requires no equipment; however there are a number of ways that you can prepare yourself and your space.

- Meditation cushion or your favorite seat

- Quiet spot that is tidy and ideally kept for meditating

- Regular time — by booking a time with yourself as you would an appointment you are more likely to keep to it

- Loose, comfortable clothes

- Turn off your phone and turn down the answering machine

- Favorite meditation technique/s

Chapter 5: Meditation

This chapter is all about the first phase in meditation. The steps involve in the first phase focused on your posture, sitting position, and focusing your mind when meditating. The first phase is the preparation of your mind and body for the process.

Choose a Comfortable Sitting Position

Meditation does not require you to follow a strict sitting position to achieve maximum results although there are positions that are recommended by veteran meditators. However, in choosing for a sitting posture, always consider your comfort and ease. Typically, you sit on a cushion on the floor/ground in a lotus position for meditation. You can also choose the half-lotus position that is much simpler than full lotus especially if your legs are not quite flexible.

If you are not comfortable sitting on the floor or ground, you can try sitting on a cushion, any chair, or bench. There are meditation benches available today but if you do not have one then there's nothing to worry about because you can still meditate by sitting on a chair.

If you decide to meditate while sitting on a chair, always observe the proper posture. To achieve the right sitting posture, start by tilting your pelvis forward; just enough for your spine to straighten or align with those last two bones in your butt where your weight is centered. You can place a 3 to 4-inch thick cushion on the edge of your seat or under the rear legs of the chair to facilitate right posture.

The most important thing to remember in determining your posture is that you should feel relaxed and comfortable throughout the meditation and not tensed or sore. Another important thing to remember is to make sure that your torso is balanced. To do this, check if your spine bears the weight of your torso, neck, and your head. If you do not feel any tension or stiffness then your torso is well balanced to facilitate proper breathing.

Remember though that whatever position you choose; you will really feel some tension especially when the sitting posture is new to you. Whenever you feel muscle tension, it is okay to relax the area where tension is felt and assess your posture. Observe if you can rebalance your torso and if you can, do so to attain a comfortable position.

After achieving a good sitting posture, a proper hand placement follows. Place your right hand on top of your left hand, palms facing upward and you should feel no pressure along your shoulder or any area that surrounds your shoulders. You can also choose to place your hands on top of your knees and just let it rest there, palms upward.

Achieving a good posture will allow you to breathe easily as your lungs will have more space for air. You have to observe how the muscles in your torso, your pelvis, muscles in your neck, and your diaphragm are working together. Part of meditation is focusing on the flow of air throughout your body so make sure that there will be no blockage as you inhale and exhale.

Close Your Eyes

Meditation can be performed with your eyes open or half-closed. However, as you are still beginning to practice this relaxation technique, it may be best to try meditating with your eyes closed. Closing your eyes during meditation helps block any external visual stimuli that may distract you as you keep your mind calm. When you close your eyes, slowly detach yourself from the environment around you, try focusing in the darkness and on your thoughts.

Once you get used to meditation with your eyes shut, you can slowly try to practice meditation with your eyes open. Open-eye meditation is helpful if you tend to fall asleep during meditation. This is quite common for people who aren't used to the practice or prefer to meditate at night when they're too tired.

If you opt for meditating with your eyes open, remember to keep your gaze soft by not to focusing on anything in particular. However, you do not have to be in a trance-like state because in meditation, you should be relaxed but alert and not hypnotic.

Stop Thinking and Start Focusing

When you close your eyes, you should stop thinking of all your worries and instead focus your attention on what you are doing. Do not entertain the thoughts or the noise your brain is fussing about. To focus, start to center your attention on the top of your head while sitting still. And as you do this, you might feel a tingling sensation on your fingers and spine. Try not to focus on those sensations since you are trying to experience thoughtlessness.

While it is important that you really focus during meditation, you may find it difficult as you are still getting the hang of meditating. Do not get too disappointed if your first meditation session is not very successful and you think you were not able to focus fully because this is understandable and quite normal for all beginners. Besides, all meditation practitioners started battling their thoughts but eventually improved through practice. If they are able to improve, so can you.

If your thoughts come ranting in your mind while you are starting to drift away, then do not let it overwhelm you. Although you can recognize the thoughts, do not let it snatch you from meditation; acknowledge the thought, slowly let it go, and shift your focus back in meditation. It usually helps to focus on something understated and continuous. For example, you can tune in to the frequency of your breathing, focusing only on the movement of your chest as you breathe in and out. This helps you tune out everything else completely. More on this will be discussed on the next chapter.

Chapter 6: Types Of Meditation

There are several different forms of meditation. The best bet is to go for the type of meditation that is simple and effective for your current life circumstances. Generally, there are two broad types of meditation:

1) Concentrative meditation: This form of meditation involves focusing your mind on a certain object, mantra, sound, or sensation. You may, for instance, focus your mind on your inhalation and exhalation, a candle flame, or even the sound of a mantra. Eventually, with repeated practice, your mind becomes calm and a space of relaxation, ease and clarity emerges. If you have never done any form of meditation before, don't panic if your thoughts keeping running wild. This is normal. Simply continue observing the breath or object.

2) Mindfulness meditation: This form of meditation involves concentrating on the mental movie happening inside. It does not include an external focal point like in concentrative meditation, but rather witnessing silently the constant thought patterns in your mind, the sensations in your body, and the stance of your emotions. This form of meditation is slightly more advanced, and calls for a great deal of non judgment and passive observance of yourself, as well as a global perspective of your mind.

Meditation techniques for stress relief

Meditation has a tremendous positive effect on overall health and stress management. While there are several different types of meditations that work well, each has its own unique effect, and some may feel more comfortable to you than others. Stick with the meditation techniques that feel right because these are the ones you will continue practicing. Here are some of the most effective, enjoyable and widely used meditation techniques for stress relief.

Chocolate Meditation

This is one of the most pleasurable types of mindfulness meditation, and it's very convenient as well. Chocolate meditation is as beneficial as any other form of meditation, but it's easier to commit to because it is designed with a reward beyond the health benefits of meditation – chocolate.

Steps

Of course, you will need a piece of chocolate for this meditation. A small piece of dark chocolate with a high concentration of cocoa is recommended, but you can also use a couple of semi sweet chips, a chocolate kiss, or anything else you have on hand.

Next, relax your body by taking in a few deep breaths. You want to be as physically calm as possible when starting the chocolate meditation. Close your eyes if it helps make you feel comfortable.

Now, bite into a small piece of your chocolate, and allow it to sit on your tongue until it melts in your mouth. Pay attention to the chocolate flavors as you become completely absorbed in what you are experiencing at the moment. Continue breathing deeply and focusing on the sensations in your mouth.

Start swallowing the chocolate, focusing on how it feels as it goes down. Observe how it leaves an empty feeling in your mouth. Now, as you take the second bite, try noticing how the chocolate feels between your fingers, how your arm feels as you raise it to your mouth, and how it feels in your mouth. Once again, pay attention to the sensations you are experiencing right now.

If other thoughts pop into your mind when meditating, gently shift back your focus to the sensations and flavors related to the chocolate. The point is to stay in the present moment for as long as possible.

Enjoy this feeling. Once you are done with the meditation (basically when the chocolate is done), revisit this feeling throughout the day to feel more relaxed. You can decide to keep on meditating after the chocolate is over, or you can simply resume with your day immediately afterwards.

The Loving Kindness Meditation

This is one of the most popular forms of meditation. The idea behind loving kindness meditation is to concentrate loving and benevolent energy towards yourself and others. The advantages of this form of meditation are clear. When you practice it with yourself as the focal point, you learn to increase feelings of self love and self acceptance, thus reinforcing more positive thinking patterns. When you use your friends and family as the subjects, you expand the circle of this meditation to include feelings of kindness towards others, and all humanity in general. You can also use loving kindness meditation to foster forgiveness towards yourself and others.

Steps

Find a quiet place and a time where you are least likely to be disturbed and sit comfortably. With your eyes closed, allow your muscles to relax, and take in a few deep breaths.

Picture yourself experiencing perfect emotional and physical wellness, as well as inner peace. Envision perfect love for yourself, being grateful to yourself for everything that you are, acknowledging that you are just fine as you are.

Think of three or four positive and reassuring phrases, and repeat them to yourself. A few examples that work include:

"May I be strong, peaceful and healthy"

"May I experience happiness"

"May I appreciate and be appreciated today"

"May I stay out of harm's way"

Dwell in that feeling for a few minutes. If you find your attention drifting to something else, gently bring it back to these emotions of loving kindness.

You can decide to focus on this mindset for the duration of your meditation, or you can shift your focus to your love ones. Start with someone you adore very much. It could be a best friend, a parent, a child, or a spouse. Feel your love and gratitude for them, and stay in that feeling. Here are some phrases you could repeat that will trigger feelings of loving kindness:

"May you be strong, peaceful and healthy"
"May you experience happiness"
"May you appreciate others and be appreciated today"
"May you stay out of harm's way"

Once these feelings have been associated with that person, bring other significant people in your life into focus, one by one, envisioning them with inner peace and perfect wellness, and then branch out to other family members and friends, acquaintances and neighbors, and so on. Including those you have a conflict with, in your meditation, can help you reach a place of greater peace or forgiveness.

When you are done with the meditation, open your eyes and keep in mind that you can revisit those wonderful feelings anytime during the day.

49

Bath Meditation

There are several different ways to experience the positive effects of meditation, and one soothing technique is to do it in the bath. A bath meditation incorporates the basic benefits of meditation with the benefits of a hot, soothing bath, which can provide a relaxing atmosphere, relax exhausted muscles, and provide a temporary feeling of freedom from your stressors.

Steps

Make time - Set aside fifteen minutes when you are least likely to be interrupted. This means setting your phone to voicemail, incorporating a few extra minutes into your schedule, and informing other members of your household not to interrupt you unless it is an emergency.

Use aromatherapy products - Incorporating bubble bath oils scented with peppermint, lavender or any other preferred scent into your bath can increase the benefits of stress relief.

Join in and relax - Allow your breathing to become deeper and slower with your belly rising and falling with every breath, as opposed to your chest or shoulders. This mode of breathing is more natural, and can go a long way towards turning off your stress response if it was prompted earlier in the day.

Focus on sensations - Pay attention to the sensations you are experiencing in your body (the pressure of the tub, the warmth of the water) and let go of any other thought. Try to calm your mind and focus your attention only on the present moment.

Stay in the present moment - If thoughts about the past, future, or any other form of internal dialogue occur, gently shift back your attention to the present moment. Keep doing this for several minutes and you will feel calm and relaxed soon.

Body Scan Meditation

When you are feeling stressed out, it is common for stress to manifest itself in your body in the form of shallow breathing, stomach "knots", tense shoulders, and various others ways. People who carry stress in their bodies are usually not aware of it. When you are feeling stressed, you may experience physical discomfort, but fail to associate it with your emotions. Body scan meditation is a form of meditation you can perform every day to help you identify what you're feeling, where you are feeling it, and learn to let go of the stress in your mind and body.

Steps

Find a comfortable place where you are less likely to be disturbed, and relax your body completely. Allow your breathing to slow down, and then start taking in deep breaths from your belly, as opposed to your chest.

Start with your head, and notice any tension you may be feeling as you practice this meditation. Do you feel any pain or tightness anywhere? Or a feeling of focused energy around a particular area? Dwell on it for a minute and observe what you are feeling.

Focus on any uncomfortable sensations you might notice. Breathe deeply into them, and observe what happens. For many people, the sensation becomes more intense at first, and then dissipates as they continue meditating and maintaining their focus. Keep you focus on that feeling a bit longer, simply staying in the present. If you want to, you can massage that area for a little while.

Move to your neck, and repeat the steps outlined above. Notice if there is any pain, pressure or tightness, and breathe into those areas as you reflect on the sensations. Give your neck a little massage if you wish to, and allow for the energy settle.

Repeat this exercise with every part of your body, moving systematically from head to toe. Observe the sensations you are experiencing, where you are holding your stress, and how you feel as a result. Continue breathing, meditating, massaging, and relaxing. This will help you release the tension in your body, and increase its awareness in the future so you can be able to release it then as well.

Walking Meditation

This is one of the best stress management techniques as it is accompanied with several varied benefits. Walking meditation is especially helpful because it combines the benefits of exercise with the benefits of meditation, and is also very easy to learn.

Steps

Get into comfortable shoes and clothing, and set aside some time where you are less likely to be disturbed.

Start by walking at a comfortable pace, really focusing on the sensations you experience in your body. Feel your body's weight at the bottom of your feet, and your arms swinging to and fro with every stride. If other thoughts pop into your mind, gently shut them out, and shift your focus back to the sensations you are experiencing as you walk.

You can also bring your breathing to your awareness while walking. For instance, try breathing in for 2 steps and out for 2 or 3 steps. Each breath in and out can be every

3 Or 4 steps or even more, whatever feels more comfortable to you. Concentrate on keeping your steps and your breathing in coordination.

Again, if you find thoughts of money, work, or other stressors pop into your mind, acknowledge their presence, and gently shift back your attention to the present, to your meditation. It is ideal to practice this for thirty minutes, several days a week, but even ten or five minutes is better than not doing it at all. You can reap the benefits of walking meditation even in small doses.

Another very effective technique to incorporate while walking is to just smile and simultaneously look up. A university study showed that participants who followed these simple steps felt much happier and more positive all around. (CAUTION: Make sure to still be aware of your surroundings while you're walking and looking up.)

Mantra Meditation

This is one of the simplest and easiest meditation techniques to learn. It carries many stress relief and wellness benefits, just like other forms of meditation, with an added bonus of ease of learning. Mantra meditation can help you feel less stressed after a single session. Repeated practice can help you become less reactive to stress in the future.

Steps

Get into a comfortable position - It is usually best to create a few minutes in your schedule and find a quiet room that is free of distraction before starting. However, with repeated practice, you may be able to carry out mantra meditation anywhere.

Select a mantra for your meditation - A mantra is simply a phrase or word that you repeat to yourself. It could be something sensible such as "I am at peace", or "Calm", or a non sensible sound such as "Om". The sounds or words you select are not very significant, as long as they are comfortable and simple for you to repeat.

Repeat the mantra to yourself with your eyes closed. As you do this, try to maintain your focus only on the sound and feeling of your mantra. If other thoughts try to creep into your mind, acknowledge their presence without judgment, and gently shift back your focus to your mantra.

Carry on for several minutes - Just continue repeating the mantra, and focusing on the sound, as well as the feeling associated with the sound. Shift your attention away from any distractions, and bring it back to your mantra. Practice with five or ten minute sessions, and then work up to twenty or thirty minutes.

Five Minute Meditation

Many people tend to ignore meditation because they think it is difficult to practice. Others believe that it is only effective with lengthy and regular sessions, but this is a false assumption. While it is true that you can experience the most benefits of meditation with regular practice, even five minutes of meditation can actually result in quick stress relief. Here is how you can make five minutes of your time count with meditation. Set a time for five minutes to avoid worrying about staying for too long in meditation and missing your appointments.

Steps

With your eyes closed, relax, and breathe in deeply from your diaphragm, releasing the tension in your body.

Let go of any thoughts in your mind. Instead of concentrating on thinking of nothing, concentrate on being in the present, and when distractive thoughts pop into your mind, acknowledge them gently, and let them go. Shift your focus back to the present moment.

Continue doing this for five minutes, and then get back to your day feeling refreshed and more relaxed.

Chapter 7: Emotional Meditation

Yes, your mind and your emotions could actually work together. Some others call this the act of rewiring one's brain. Just imagine how life would be like if you actually get to control your emotions, and not succumb to them, simply by allowing yourself to get lost in them for a moment and then moving on.

Studies show that the emotional circuits of one's brain are actually connected to the brain's thinking circuits. In fact, cognition is also considered to have a lot to do with emotions—and that is why you definitely are stronger than you think.

The thing is, people have often been told that the mind and the heart are two different things, and that the mind controls the emotions. What people fail to realize is that the mind, especially the hypothalamus, is actually responsible for dealing with emotions!

Emotional Meditation Exercise:

Meanwhile, here's what you can do to practice emotional meditation:

1.   Upon being aware of an emotion, stop, and feel it for a while. Let it consume you for a while. For example, if you're frustrated because you feel like your hard work is not paying off, allow yourself to feel that pain. Allow yourself to be frustrated, or to get angry even. Do not inhibit your feelings or suppress them—things will get worse that way.

2.   Next, identify the emotions that you feel. If you are heartbroken, feel it. Say you have been hurt badly, and that you hate what you're feeling. Again, it's always better to recognize the emotion rather than be numb, or pretend that it is not happening.

3.   Open yourself up to what you're feeling. Don't even think about what lead you there anymore, or why things happened. Life is always that way, you know? You never really get to understand why things happen. For example, if a relationship failed, it's not because you

62

have not done enough. Things just happen. Period. Focus on what you feel and don't try to dumb it down—so that someday, you can move on.

4. Realize that emotions are temporary. As you're feeling what you're feeling, remind yourself that it will pass, but while it's there, ask yourself how you can help yourself get through it. Sadness could be channeled into poems or novels. Maybe, you could write your feelings out to exorcise them. It's all a matter of introspection, you see.

5. Finally, when you are calm enough, and when you see that your emotions are real, you could investigate and see why they happened, or why you still feel them. If you are still in pain about losing someone form 3 years back, maybe, you still have not fully moved on. When you get to understand this, you also begin to know what to do to help yourself get out of that rut. Maybe, you need a change of friends? A change of scenery? If you are still mad at the person who broke your heart, are you still going to confront him?

Or would you rather just cut of all ties with him, and move on? It's now the time for you to choose the appropriate response for this.

6.　　Be open to what happens next. Remember that your emotions do not have to define you—you can always move on from them, and now is the time to do so.

Chapter 8: Beyond Probiotics: How

Meditation Heals The Gut

Why do You Have Two Brains?

The answer lies in how mindfulness heals your gut better than probiotics, and the powerful "emotion⇆ stomach" connection.

"Trust your intuition, trust your gut... I'm so nervous, I have butterflies in my stomach... I have a gut feeling to reject this job offer... What a gut-wrenching experience."

This link is now showing up in many cool and interesting scientific ways. With more than 100 million nerves lining your so called "second brain," the gut / enteric nervous system (ENS) is actually composed of the very same tissue(s) as your central nervous system (CNS).

Why The "Gut-Brain Axis" Is Essential To Health

In fact, many doctors are now saying that our deeply intertwined "first" real brain and "second" gut brain (sometimes called the gut-brain axis) are actually one system, not two.

While it can't do calculus, write a novel, or pass an exam — your gut certainly can orchestrate a symphony of neurotransmitters, hormones, and electrical impulses.

Beyond helping you digest food, your gut has its own brain-like neural network, playing critical roles in keeping you healthy, including regulating inflammation and commanding your immune system.

So, will simply eating right keep the gut-brain axis in balance? Not necessarily. Here we will go into why your state of mind is so critical to gut health, and why meditation is the missing link above and beyond diet.

Why the Mind Is Key to a Healthy Gut

To illustrate the mind-gut link, have you ever heard of the guy afflicted with the "incurable, unknown origin" chronic disease? After visiting a dozen or so doctors, they all have one simple but bewildering diagnosis: "it's all in your head"! This is a common occurrence as it happens more often than we think.

In fact, gastroenterologists have compiled more than 20 of these "all in your head" GI tract diseases (FGIDs), which account for the vast majority of clinical visits.

So, what're the reasons for these mysterious illnesses? Diet? No, because many of these folks have already tried everything, and why the doctor has labeled their affliction effectively "psychosomatic."

Why your Ability To Handle Stress Controls the Gut-Brain Axis

The culprit is a known offender, sitting atop the health police's most wanted list — stress.

How to perfect your gut health using the power of your mind

Even after switching to a healthy diet, stress explains why many "second brain" gut-related diseases still stick around.

Strengthening the link, research has shown that psychological trauma can lead to digestive problems, inflammation, ulcers, IBS, IBD, Crohns, & more.

In light of these new findings, it is obvious that healing the gut is impossible without addressing our ability to manage emotion and stress. How you think does affect your health.

How To Heal Your Gut With Your Mind: Meditation heals the gut without probiotics

As the #1 stress conqueror, meditation is the top contender for the "gut-health" championship belt. Who are the other competitors in the ring, duking it out? Probiotics, psychobiotics, diet, and prescription drugs.

(Note: Boxing metaphor aside, when it comes to your highest health, all of the above options certainly have their rightful place, of course.)

Here is one study firmly planted in meditation's corner:

Study: How Meditation Turns off "Bad" Gut Genes, While Helping 1,000+ More

For 48 patients suffering irritable bowel syndrome (IBD) and inflammatory bowel disease (IBD), a 9 week study at Massachusetts General Hospital changed everything.

Meditation had somehow managed to beneficially alter more than 1,000 genes, including suppressing the nasty protein complex arsonist (NF-kB) responsible for igniting (inflaming) the immune system and GI tract.

Your gut is incredibly important for overall health. Diet, while important, does not guarantee a healthy microbiome. As evidenced by the "gut-brain-axis," your ability to handle stress is (arguably) more important than diet, along with genes.

Luckily, meditation not only dominates stress like Michael Jordan over the '92-'93

Phoenix Suns, but also orchestrates a Mozart-like symphony expressing only your "cream of the crop" genes.

Become Superhuman: How "The Iceman" Wim Hof Used Meditation To Become Superhuman

Harness Your Mind, Achieve Frozen Feats

Results Are In: The Wim Hof method put to the test by researchers

Maybe you caught The "Iceman" Wim Hof on a National Geographic documentary, viral Youtube video, or Discovery Channel feature. Now living legends, news of his jaw-dropping accomplishments have spread far and wide.

An holder of more than 25 Guinness World Records, the nearly 60 year old dutchman has become renowned for his ability to withstand extremely cold temperatures by using meditation to crank up his "inner thermostat."

Before we tell you the massive implications of his "superhuman" abilities, here are a few of his frozen feats:

How Wim Hof's meditation method makes him superhuman

Braving hurricane force wind chills (-53°C, -63°F), in 2007 the Iceman climbed the world's tallest peak, Mt Everest, wearing only shorts. Two years later, National Geographic & the BBC filmed him run a barefoot marathon in the Arctic Circle (-20°C, -4°F).

Packed head to toe with 1000+ pounds of ice, Wim Hof can last two full hours effectively "frozen." He has broken his own "full ice immersion" record 6+ times on various TV appearances.

He has done a lot of other cool stuff, too. But you get the idea.

How The Iceman Makes The Impossible, Possible. Mind Over Matter: A Few Studies

How the Iceman's meditation method manipulates his immune system

How does he do it? To raise his body temperature, the dutchman manipulates his autonomic nervous system (ANS) through deep meditative breathing techniques. Therein lies the controversy.

The human autonomic nervous system is, according to to all medical textbooks, involuntary and therefore — impossible to consciously manipulate and control. The lungs, kidney, liver, and heart work all by themselves or so they say.

The Iceman's meditation method revealed

But the data is now suggesting otherwise. While the Iceman is the ultimate "mind over matter" case study, other researchers have discovered similar remarkable abilities in trained meditators.

Author of "Counter Clockwise" and Harvard Professor, Ellen Langer has shown that we can consciously slow and speed our heart rate after only one week of mindfulness training.

Legendary Mind-Body researcher and author of the best-selling book "Relaxation Response," Dr. Herbert Benson found that meditating monks could increase the temperature of their fingers and toes by as much as 47°F (8.3°C), while drying wet blankets through mental control of their body heat!

The point is that, yes, we most certainly can do things with our mind and body that science once believed impossible.

The Iceman's Immunity Put To The Test

The Wim Hof breathing method: Using meditation for superhuman health and immunity

Can the Iceman, with his superhuman abilities, also ward off disease?

To test's Hof's conscious immune system control, researchers at Radboud University Nijmegen Medical Centre injected him with an endotoxin (bacteria) which causes flu-like symptoms and inflammation.

What did the doctors find? The test results showed that the injected bacteria had zero impact on the Iceman. In other words, his meditation fueled immune system forced the pathogen into submission. Pretty amazing.

But the question then becomes, is Wim Hof just a freak of nature, one in a billion, an extreme outlier?

From "Average Joe" To "Superhuman": The Iceman Trains 12 Students

The Wim Hof method: Using meditation for super health and immunity

Wim says that his feats and superman abilities are available to anyone and everyone who practices his meditative techniｺues. Intrigued by the possibility, researchers put his claim to the test.

For 10 days, Wim trained 12 students with the very same deep breathing meditative techniｺue that he practices.

In the lab his meditators were injected with dead E. coli bacteria, which invokes the same immuno-response as a living pathogen.

And The Researchers Were Astonished

The Iceman Wim Hof's student immunity test results

The meditators showed little to no effects from the injection, quickly squashing any flulike symptoms and inflammation.

How did they do it? By "breathing" high levels of oxygen into their blood, the meditators triggered a cataclysm of immuno-upgrades, starting with better tissue alkalinity and elevated levels of adrenaline/epinephrine.

(Note: An acidic body is linked to countless diseases. Luckily, meditation makes the body more alkaline, as this study clearly shows.)

Study author Matthijs Kox, told LiveScience: "The adrenaline levels were higher than in people who bungee jumped for the first time...The acid-base [blood] balance oxygen levels... could lead to this effect."

Harnessing Neuroplasticity: How Meditation Builds Healthy, Immune Brains

Scientific Breakthrough: We Can Now "Sculpt" Our Brain

Neuroplasticity, health, & immunity

Your brain's potential is "fixed" at birth. Mom and dad's brain genes transferred to your DNA double helix determine your grades, SAT score, career path, and how much money you make. Is this true?

Note: While scientists' were once convinced that we could not upgrade our brain throughout life, recent discoveries have proven otherwise.

Neuroplasticity and boosting health

By taking a jackhammer to once carved in stone medical dogma, the brain's newly discovered "neuroplastic" nature means that we can carve and mold our noggin' like a sculptor shapes his clay.

That is, through certain types of activities, we can physically and functionally change and upgrade our brains in ways once believed impossible.

Why Meditation Is the "Michelangelo" Of Brain Sculpting

How mindfulness changes the brain, boosts immunity, and benefits health

In her best-selling book, "You Are Not Your Brain," Rebecca Gladding MD recently wrote "The brain, and how we are able to mold it, is fascinating and nothing short of amazing."

Then, what's the best way to upgrade the human brain? With thousands of studies fueling the movement, many scientists believe meditation to be the best way to build a better, healthier brain.

Helping to ward off would-be invaders, here are four immune system linked brain regions that meditation so conveniently fortifies.

Meditation Brain Region #1 — Insula Cortex: Why Compassionate People Are So Healthy

Neuroplasticity: How to build a compassionate brain for super health and immunity

A highly cited 2008 University of Wisconsin study showed the empathy linked "insula cortex" to be very active while a meditator is "in session.

What's the link? Many studies, including one at Emory University School of Medicine, have shown that compassionate people have, along with huge reductions in inflammation, better stress responses and far healthier immune systems.

Think of the kindest people that you know. According to scientists, they should also be the healthiest that you know.

New meditators often report a big "shift" in consciousness very early in their regimen. Is awakening their dormant "insula cortex" the reason for this upgrade? Quite possibly.

Meditation Brain Region #2 — Hippocampus: "King Hippo" Drops Depression

Neuroplasticity & the Hippocampus: Less depression for a healthier brain and body

People with depression know this brain region well. Actually, maybe they don't, because depression grinds the hippocampus down to a nub. Luckily, meditation reverses the atrophy, making it big and strong again.

A 2008 UCLA study (Neuroimage Journal) found that after only 8 weeks of practice, meditators had physically and functionally grown the neural thickness, density, and overall size of their "right hippocampi".

With dementia, heart disease, cancer, and thyroid problems topping the list of depression related diseases, meditation's implied health upgrading capacity is truly mind-boggling.

Meditation Brain Region #3 — Prefrontal Cortex: Build Intelligence & Health

Neuroplasticity & the Prefrontal Cortex: How the Einstein Brain elevates health

If all of the brain regions held an election, then the Prefrontal Cortex would be emperor.

Perhaps the greatest dividing line between neanderthals and modern man, this "king of all brain regions" is ruler for good reason, known for zapping anxiety and depression, good decision making, high intelligence (like Albert Einstein), strong immune system function, and more.

Neuroplasticity & the Prefrontal Cortex: How being smart boosts the immune system

Then, what's the best way to build up the prefrontal cortex?

In 2005, a groundbreaking study by esteemed Harvard neuroscientist Dr. Sara Lazar found that meditation practitioners had extremely "well-developed" prefrontal cortexes, with a direct link between experience and size, strength, and "folds" (gyrification).

So, meditation not only fortifies your immune system, it can supercharge your intellect. Win win.

Meditation Brain Region #4 — The Amygdala: Achieve Stress Mastery

Neuroplasticity & The Amygdala: How to lower stress by changing the brain

With countless studies implying that stress causes nearly every disease, it becomes clear that less stress leads to more health. You don't need to be a doctor to see that the sky is blue.

Responsible for the "caveman" fear response within the brain, modern man is activating his double-almond sized "amygdala" way too often.

How many times did you face a life or death situation last month? Are you fighting lions, tigers, and bears on your daily commute to work? (Depending on the traffic in your city this may actually be true!)

The amygdala: How mindfulness lowers the stress response and changes the brain

The problem is our primitive caveman amygdala is triggering negative stress hormones in response to our job problems, financial difficulties, and relationship squabbles. You can take the "caveman out of the cave", but you can't take the "cave out of the caveman".

Or can we? Is it possible to evolve this primitive brain region, and in essence, hack ourselves to the front of the evolution queue? Yes, through meditation!

As evidenced by countless studies (including an 8 week Massachusetts General Hospital MRI brain scan study), the "caveman" stress response brain region, the amygdala, is cooled off and deactivated in and after meditation.

By shrinking the brain's fear center, your stress plummets, and your health and immune system soar.

Cure Headaches: People who practice meditation reap many great benefits, including the alleviation of so many mental, emotional, and physical problems.

Specific to physical health, meditation is widely acclaimed for strengthening the immune system, lessening sickness fre?uency, and promoting faster healing. However, not everyone knows that it can also readily alleviate chronic conditions — especially headaches and migraines.

Here are 5 important things to understand:

1. Meditation has been scientifically proven to reduce headaches. This understanding is backed up by the research of Herbert Benson (M.D.), Helen P. Klemchuck (A.B.) and John R Graham (M.D.) who found that regularly practicing meditation can reduce headache incidents by at least 37%, and that certain forms of meditation have been shown to

completely eliminate headaches in some individuals over the long term. Another example of cold hard science confirming age old meditation wisdom.

2.   Muscle tension & subconscious clenching cause headaches, meditation fixes both. Headaches is often caused by bodily tension, especially when that tension is held in the face, jaw and neck. Meditation is the very best way to relax your whole body, from the tip of your toes to the top of your head. As you sink into a meditative trance, you naturally release all headache causing culprits. By not subconsciously tensing up over every thought, you reduce the chances of developing a headache, while increasing the chance of being able to eliminate a headache quickly after it develops.

3.   Natural cures, like meditation, are best in the short and long term. Society has a natural tendency, especially in recent years, to seek out natural cures

rather than popping a pill. For people who regularly suffer from headaches & migraines, anything that can help is all but a miracle, and the fact that meditation is such a simple and easy natural headache cure makes it that much better.

4. Mind mastery is where the meditative journey leads. Meditation allows you to let go of all toxic mental conditions, moving into the present moment, finding that calm and quiet space within where there is nothing to worry about. This is where mind masters (long time meditators) spend their time. When free of anxiety, depression, worry, & other headache causing emotions, you become free to live your life, fulfilling much greater levels of your potential.

5. Fewer Free Radicals: he Inner Antioxidant: How Meditation Reduces Free Radicals. A free radical is an agent which attacks our cells from the inside-out. To understand how we must

understand that our cells are made up of atoms with a nucleus at the center. This nucleus is surrounded by a cloud of negatively charged particles called electrons, which work in pairs.

For many reasons, including stress, depression, and environmental factors, an atom in one of our cells may lose an electron. The loss of an electron is how an atom becomes a free radical, which can now attack the cell it occupies, damaging and eventually killing it.

Death and damage in our cells is exactly what aging is, the solution – antioxidants. Antioxidants are nutrients made in the human body and found in healthy foods. Antioxidants donate their extra electrons to free radicals restoring balance.

The human body can produce its own antioxidants, but with the activities we do daily, and the toxins we are exposed to in food and in the environment, we rupture more cells than we can produce. This is especially so if we do not get adequate sleep, are over-stressed, anxious, or depressed, which is why meditation helps fight free radicals.

Meditation restores restful and peaceful states to the mind, relaxing muscles, oxygenating blood, and increasing the flow of nutrients to cells, so the body can naturally produce antioxidants.

The body gets more quality time to heal while meditating than while sleeping. When sleeping, your brain is still thinking subconsciously, as is manifesting itself in dreams. During meditation, this isn't the case. During meditation your mind is relaxed, giving your body the energy to boost your immune system, fight disease, and produce antioxidants.

The result is increased longevity, better health, and an increased quality of life. By slowing the aging process and fighting free radicals, we reduce our risks of cancer and disease. Meditation is the fountain of youth we have all been waiting for, and it is available to you right now. All you have to do is get started.

Chapter 9: What Is The Mantra, And Why Is It Needed?

Do you know why the Japanese are the most intelligent nation in the world? It's because they have the greatest number of vowels in their speech, compared with other languages. It is scientifically proven that the pronunciation of certain sound sequences can be administered to a person in a certain state, to adjust their health and cure disease through improving the functioning of certain organs. Indian yogis knew about it a long time ago, and in each case have come up with a sequence of sounds, called a mantra. But the mantra is not only from the Indian yogis. This practice is present in almost all the nations of the world. For example, prayer is also a mantra. Mantra reading plunges you into a certain state, but not only the reader, but also the listener.

The human body, like any other being has its own vibration. Every organ has its own vibration. If a person utters a sound, then the sound may coincide with the organ vibration and configure it, but if a failure has occurred in an organ and disrupted the vibration – the body is sick.

The mantra is the spoken sequence of sounds that is perceived not only by sensory organs, but all organs of the body. The most common and universal mantra is the mantra OM. Pay attention to some subtleties of its execution and effect.

When performing meditation, we take a deep breath, imagining how is pouring into us a stream clear blue glowing pure energy (prana). Prana first fills your lungs from the bottom up, flooding from above like a mist. Then it concentrates in the solar plexus.

1.   When you pronounce the sound Ah-Ah-Ah, you feel the vibration in your chest at the level of the solar plexus.

Practical use: vibration in the solar plexus affects the nerves, harmonizing the energy of the whole body.

2.   Then gradually move to the sound Oh-Oh-Oh, concentrating on the chest in the heart area.

Practical use: vibration of the sound Oh-Oh-Oh affects the bone structure of the thorax, the lungs, improves gas exchange.

3.   Change to the sound of OO-OO-OO and move the vibration to the throat and lower part of the skull.

Practical use: vibration in the throat activates the thyroid gland and has a calming effect on the body.

4.   As you finish, the vibration gradually shifts attention and direction to the top of your head with the sound, M-M-M.

Practical use: the activation of the entire brain, lifts depression, decreases inferiority complexes and awakens the senses.

The whole body enters a state of inner harmony.

When you perform mantras, it has a very powerful the effect of the rest of the body, so it is highly recommended for busy people. Precisely because of its high

89

efficiency, the system of transcendental meditation is so common worldwide, in spite of the high cost of guru services.

A lot more could be written about the practical benefits of the OM mantra. But words cannot really convey the experience of sensations, so I have only given you the correct recommendations for you to try, do, meditate. The effect will not take long after the first class.

The mantra of OM is versatile and absolutely safe, but the following mantra should be approached carefully. These mantras have a real and strong effect, but if one doesn't fit and you feel uncomfortable, it's better to avoid it.

With weak retrosternal chest pain and hypertension there should be 1-5 minutes of stretching and chanting of the sounds Z-U-M-M-E-I or H-R-A-M. They are pronounced in a low tone of voice.

For mild sclerosis of the vessels, with a mid-tone of voice, say P-A-A-A—Ee-Ee-Ee

Disturbances in the respiratory system recover with the Mantra P-A-A-A-S-S-S.

Digestive function is restored with P-O-U-P-O-U

To strengthen the nervous system well chant M-P-O -M-P-E

Chapter 10: People Very Rarely Have The

Time To Sit Still Anymore

Let's face it, people very rarely have the time to sit still anymore.

Or at least that's what we like to tell ourselves.

The real truth, the part that most people don't like to admit, is that if you don't have time you can always make it. It isn't really a problem of lack of time so much as it is the lack of motivation and creativity. Meditation isn't something you have to set a reminder for on your phone so that you do it on time. Nor is it a chore that you have to cancel plans and work for. It's something that you can engage in when moments present themselves. Which they do more often than not.

You can call it 'personal care', 'me time', or even a 'mental health day'.

No matter what you call it, the point is that you have to take time out for yourself no matter the chaos going on around you.

Taking time doesn't equate to going to the beach, the movies, or shopping. That's a different type of self-care altogether. What I'm referring to requires more of a mental step back than a physical one. Though, you can certainly combine the two.

A mental retreat is simple enough to accomplish and can be done anywhere at any time. When you're taking a shower or bath (assuming you don't have the time for a bath) is the perfect opportunity to practice. You can also try on the go meditation when you're riding the elevator, sitting down for lunch, during your commute to work while you're stuck in traffic, or while you're taking a 15-minute break or 30-minute lunch.

If you find that you need a mental pick up before a long day or after finally getting home after a particularly tough one, try to meditate in that window of time that comes right before you close your eyes and right after waking. It's that moment where you aren't quite ready for the world yet but sleep hasn't let you go. It can be as brief or as long as you need it to be. Just tailor that moment for yourself and revel in it.

You don't have to complete a specific form of meditation from start to finish in order to reap the full effects of it. Most people who practice on a regular basis are able to streamline the process so that they can touch on succinct points and use them to their advantage. For instance, the peace that can come about during the midst of meditation can be captured with timed breathing and a very deliberate mental break. It's a lot like a parent stepping to one side and taking a deep breath while they count to ten. It helps to reorganize the thoughts and get a firm grasp on emotions that may have been getting out of control.

It's important to remember that you run your body, not the other way around.

Sometimes that means treating yourself like the parent and your emotions like recalcitrant children. Like children they have little control over themselves, don't require thought or reason in order to act, and are selfish in a way that speaks of not yet understanding that the world does not revolve for or around them. While it's important to nurture the pure idealism that they represent, you don't have to allow yourself to be bulldozed in the process.

Some confuse being in touch with their emotions without being controlled by them. While this is a fine line to walk, the tightrope becomes a little steadier with practice and attention. It's easier to fill in your frayed bits and pieces when you've traversed the line before and shone a light on where you've stumbled.

I get it.

You're the type of person who always finds themselves taking care of other people.

Whether you want to or not doesn't really matter. What matters is that no one can seem to get their act together unless you do it for them. You're always doubling up and doubling down to make sure that things get accomplished and maybe people don't appreciate the effort you make as much as they should.

But when the plane goes down you have to reach for your own mask first before you can help anyone else. By now the comparison must seem cliché, but clichés are born in literature for a reason. When something rings true, you use it. You can lead a horse to water but you can't make him drink. You can teach a man to fish and he will feed himself for a lifetime. You can't help someone else if you're lungs explode in the cockpit mid airplane death-spiral. It's all about perspective.

But maybe you're not the selfless parental type. Maybe you're just lonely, and sad, and more nervous than it makes sense to be and those doubts that would normally mutter like wizened old men in the back of someone else's mind always seem to scream in yours. A chance to quiet it all down to a dull roar and eventually to silence would be a weight off of your shoulders.

Or perhaps, you're neither of those people and you're just tired. Disillusioned. You aren't sure where you're going or where you want to go but you know you want to find out. You're looking for that epiphany, that 'ah ha' moment that they always have in books but it seems as if it'll never come.

You could be a professional at the top of your field, or 12-years old and too nervous to speak up at the front of the class, or a combat vet who still flinches and finds his mind wandering down grim hallways when lights flash a little too bright or when sounds are just a little too loud.

The point, which I'm sure you've picked up on by now, is that age, occupation, gender, and so forth make little difference in the scheme of things. If you've picked up this book and you've read it this far through, then you're looking for something. You may not have been able to find those answers anywhere else or perhaps you're simply searching for affirmation to something you already know. Either way, regardless of the who or the why, the answer will remain the same.

Make time for yourself. It's just as important, if not more so, as doing it for friends and family. For those who have a hard time getting into the proper mindset at the drop of a hat, there are a few ways that you can get a jumpstart.

For instance, there are several videos on YouTube dedicated to putting your mind in the right space for meditation. Binaural frequencies can be used for meditation, to increase brain function, to promote a sense of peace and love, and etc. These frequencies are based on the fact that sound waves have the ability to induce certain responses. Different frequencies are played in tandem to create special side effects. Lower and higher frequencies can be used to cancel each other out or a create a much louder experience. They can also interact with one another and play off their strengths so that they combine in new creative ways to create harmony. Each wave responds to different frequencies and each wave is responsible for certain functions of the brain.

• Beta Waves - These brain waves are associated with attentiveness, concentration and anticipation, and selective attention or focus on a specific item or idea. These are the waves responsible for solving complicated problems and generating feelings of anxiety and apprehension. These waves are for normal electrical activity within the brain. Being alert and awake places you within the Beta category. Beta brain waves respond to 12 Hz to 30 Hz frequencies and when used by experienced practitioners to meditate they have been found to induce a state of ecstasy and concentration.

• Theta Waves – These waves range along 4 Hz to 7 Hz, are witnessed when an individual is motionless but alert. They are associated with dreaming, deep meditation, hypnosis, and light sleep and are connected with short-term memory. What makes theta waves especially interesting when it comes to meditation, is that this is the state the brain can be found while people are experiencing a

99

twilight state. This is the moment when you're not really awake but not fully asleep and during this time hallucinations can occur. Scientists say that this state is best for creative problem-solving.

• Alpha Waves — These waves are associated with a deep state of relaxation and meditation and move at a frequency of 8 Hz to 12 Hz. Creative thought and a sense of relaxation and peace can be attributed to these waves. These waves are the ones most prominent during meditation and are important for relaxation. Marijuana users exhibit these waves when smoking.

• Delta Waves — Set at 0.1 Hz to 4 Hz frequencies, these waves are associated with deep stage 3, or slow wave, sleep. People don't dream in this state and the deeper the sleep the higher the delta waves. Only experienced practitioners seem to experience a meditative state while exhibiting delta waves since maintaining a level of consciousness while also deep sleep is very difficult. Those who accomplish it are usually those who are associated with or have some practice with, ancient Indian Yoga.

• Gamma Waves – set at 30 Hz and 70 Hz these waves are related to the processing of visual, audio, and touch-based stimuli. It is connected with collecting these stimuli and joining them into a coherent piece. Gamma waves play a supporting role in the brain and are seen primarily while an individual is awake. They can be seen during Buddhist meditation of compassion and during music listening experiments.

The list goes on, but these brain waves are the five main categories and each can be reactivated by outside sounds matching a similar frequency. You can focus on videos dedicated to certain frequencies or you can set up a playlist dedicated to guided meditation tracks. Your playlist can be played anywhere and it can be used as a crutch or training wheel until you get the hang of meditating on your own.

It's worth it in the long run and the benefits will far outweigh whatever disbelief you have to suspend. If you're like most people, you like to put off for tomorrow what you can do today. You do it over and over again until tomorrow just isn't there anymore. Or perhaps you give the whole thing a shot but you don't stick to it. It's a one-hit wonder in your eyes. Maybe it worked, maybe it didn't. But trying once or twice is, apparently, the epicenter of your self-sacrifice.

Don't be that person.

Give meditation a fair shot, try it over and over again until it no longer feels like a chore but a relief. You won't regret it and the extra effort will make a world of difference in your day to day life.

Chapter 11: Meditation Techniques For

Inner Peace

Gold medals to those who can make it through this book without mindlessly scrolling through Facebook, wondering about unattended emails or dinner, or scanning half a page before realizing you have no clue what on earth you just read. Some people have a name for this state: the autopilot daze, where you are physically here, but mentally elsewhere – your default mode and it is not the greatest place to be. Majority of the population spend the better half of their day in default mode, in which they are typically unhappy. Adding too much time in this state can lead to increased risk of anxiety, depression, and attention deficit. Our brains counter this default mode through the focus mode. Imagine how you'd react, if, as you were reading, a kangaroo walked up to you. It is highly likely that you would stop reading and thinking about Facebook, dinner and emails, and shift your focus entirely on the kangaroo. Of course, you may not want a kangaroo following you, but it is helpful to engage that focused attention this experience beckons. Meditation helps you to do just that – cut through your brain's static and find focus. Apart from its numerous health benefits, including stress management, possibly helping with depression, heart disease, and high blood pressure, it is also something you can tailor into your daily life. If you just want to give it a try, you don't need to take a visit to the monastery or the doctor's office. The practice is nothing mystical. It is essentially your trained attention.

If you are a beginner, you can try the 3 simple meditation exercises for inner peace explained below just about any time and any place. Just remember to go slow, and be gentle and compassionate with yourself. It is natural for your mind to wander when trying to focus, so when it does, do not distress.

Walking Meditation

This practice is relatively simple, traditional and well suited for stressed out people in the modern society. Find a suitable place outside, and walk at a slow to medium pace while focusing on your feet. Try to differentiate when your toe points back upward, when the foot falls flat on the ground, and then when your toe touches the ground. Feel as your foot rolls on the ground, and then observe sensory details – a pull of the stock here, and a tingle there. In case your attention wanders, and it will, bring back your attention gently to your feet. You are developing the skill of being aware when your attention shifts to default mode, and then bringing it back into focus. This skill can help you be more present and in control of your thoughts every day, especially when you are stressed out.

Mindfulness Meditation

The best way to describe this type of meditation is as an observation technique, where you don't really do anything. It is a very passive process where you are able to notice things, but choose not to react to them. You notice your thoughts and feelings as they occur, but rather than judging them, you simply observe and let them drift away. You are able to notice external sounds and distractions, but choose not to react to them. You simply let go of your analytical mind and allow yourself to be in the present moment, and this brings peace, clarity and insight.

*Prepare yourself by finding a calm and comfortable place where there are minimal instances of interruptions. Get a comfortable chair and sit with your feet flat on the floor and your back straight against the backrest. If you need to recline for any physical reason, feel free to do so. If you would rather sit on the floor with your legs crisscrossed, then do so as long as you are comfortable and your back is straight. Also, you should loosen any tight clothing and then take your shoes off.

*Start by allowing yourself to relax. With your eyes closed, take in some slow and deep breaths. Feel as the muscles in your body loosen, particularly the ones around your shoulders, neck, and face. Now start breathing naturally.

*Focus on your breath to keep you hooked in the present moment. Simply observe your breath and find something to note about it. It could be the contraction and expansion of your lungs, or the feeling of the air flowing through your nose. Just keep focused on the chosen aspect of your breath, but do not try too hard. The point is not to concentrate, but rather to focus gently.

*Thoughts and images will spring into your mind. Identify and acknowledge their presence, and then let them flow by. Avoid judging them or hanging onto them in any way. Be aware of when a thought comes to mind, and then gently shift your focus back to your breath. You may also notice external noises, but avoid reacting to these or starting an inner dialogue. Let them be, and shift your focus back to your breath.

*If your mind is overwhelmed with plenty of thoughts, as you will probably do when starting, do not get frustrated or angry with yourself. The goal is to allow you to be and allow whatever comes to pass without judgment or reaction.

*Spare about twenty minutes being mindful in this way. When the time is up, sit quietly for about two minutes with your eyes still closed to allow yourself to shift back to normal consciousness before carrying on with your day.

*Take notes of any other experiences or insights you may have had, but don't feel disappointed if you lack anything to write.

Regardless of what happens, you have succeeded in the technique, even if you had several thoughts. The simple fact that you let them pass away means that you have benefited from the practice.

Breathing Meditation

Breathing meditation is probably the easiest form of meditation, but don't be fooled by its simplicity. Of course, like any other type of meditation, the more practice you do, the more benefits you will gain, and the more efficient you will become. Breathing meditation uses the breath as the point of focus. Meditation is basically the conscious decision to calm the mind and focus on one thing while eliminating everything else.

*To get started, begin by finding a comfortable place to sit where you are unlikely to be disturbed. Be seated in a comfortable chair with your feet flat on the floor and your back straight against the chair. You may also sit cross legged on the floor if you like, but make sure you are comfortable and your back is straight. It is also advisable to loosen any tight clothing and take off your shoes.

*Start by closing your eyes and taking in some slow and deep breaths in order to allow yourself to relax. Feel as the muscles in your entire body loosen, especially those around your neck, shoulders, and face, and then bring your breath to a natural pace.

Counting Each Breath

This is the simplest form of the breathing meditation technique, and is simply all about counting each breath. Count "one" in your mind gently as you breathe in, and "two" while you breathe out, then "three" when you inhale again, and so forth.

*Try keeping your breath as natural and even as possible. It can be easy to exaggerate the breaths when doing this meditation and your breathing can become fast and deep.

*Count each exhalation and inhalation in a gentle natural rhythm. You can focus on whatever aspect of your breath you want when counting, such as the sensation of the air passing through your nose, or the expansion and contraction of your chest.

*You could, for example, decide to count to ten, and then restart, or simply keep counting upwards.

Counting The Out Breath Only

Keeping count of the exhalations only is slightly harder since the gaps between the counts are a bit longer. However, simply follow the procedure for counting each breath.

Follow The Breath Without Counting

This meditation technique utilizes the movements of the breath only as a point of focus, without actually counting. You can use any aspect of your breath to focus, including the rise and fall of your abdomen, the coolness of the air passing through your nostrils, and the sensation of the air going through your lungs.

Several images and thoughts are bound to spring to mind. This is very common when meditating, so simply identify and acknowledge their presence, and then allow them to pass. Avoid judging or hanging onto them. When you notice a thought occurring, just shift your focus gently to your breath.

Chapter 12: The Art Of Visualization

As you progress though these exercises, you are beginning to understand that there are many different types of techniques for meditating. As indicated, breathing is the basic tenant of all exercises. However, the decision is yours as to which specific exercise you choose to delve deeper into your state of mind and attempt to obtain inner peace and harmony. As a newcomer to meditation, or even someone who has been doing it for years, it is recommended that you try various exercises and techniques to find the one that best enables you to reach the serenity and joy we all deserve in our lives.

Another valuable tool for your meditation exercises is visualization. When utilizing concentration exercises, you opened your eyes, picked a particular item and focused all your thoughts on that specific item. You were not thinking about what the item was, what its function was, or what you could do with that item. Instead you were simply concentrating on that item.

Visualization uses your focus and concentration in a different manner.

Visualization is an exercise in your mind. You continue to master your breathing with your eyes closed. Once you have reached the point where you feel your body, mind and soul are prepared, you picture in your mind a particular place or location. One again, if you feel a connection to the spiritual world, you may want to visualize a religious place, such as a temple or church. In order to connect to the spiritual center of the body, some advocates of meditation suggest that you visualize an item as representative of your spiritual center. You focus on this visualization allowing your spiritual center to become a part of you, washing over you and giving you a sense of peace in your connection with your religion.

The location you have chosen can be based on a real place, but should be completely your own. It is a personalized reality, one that you imagine based on where you feel most at peace. Many visualize a warm sunny beach, a flower filled garden, or a cabin with a roaring fire. It does not matter what your location is, as long as its unique to you. It will become your sanctuary. It is a place you feel safe and secure, and can allow your body, mind and soul to become calm and relaxed.

As you enter your sanctuary in your mind, begin exploring the location. You will not need to invent or create the surroundings, as they will just be there. The location is in your mind and you are going wherever your mind will allow you to go in the sanctuary. You must let the scene dominate your thoughts, eliminating all ideas of any other places or activities. You must reduce your consciousness to existing solely in your sanctuary in your mind.

As you explore, absorb all the feelings associated with the location. If you are on the beach, feel the salt spray hit your face. If you are sitting in the cabin, get the sensation of warmth flowing from the fire. If you are in the garden, take in the beautiful smells, fragrances, and sights of the luscious environment. Wherever you are in your mind, allow yourself to feel the warm breeze caress your body as you walk in your sanctuary. This is a location of complete safety and security, a place where tension and anxiety do not exist. You want your body to arrive at a state of meditation where the entire feeling of serenity and tranquility of your sanctuary encompasses your whole being, mind , body and soul.

As with all meditation exercises, the choices are yours as to the duration and length. If you feel you have reached a good place, you can take some deep breathes and open your eyes. This can last for a few minutes or longer. You should explore the location for as long as it feels natural, as long as it grows in your mind. Some beginners may not want to try this at the start, as submersing yourself in a visualized sanctuary sometimes is not easy. We can begin to imagine all sorts of other activities and things going on at the beach, or in the garden, or at the cabin. This is not the purpose. You are not inventing scenarios, but choosing a sanctuary where you can just explore, experience, and live.

A good method to employ n your exercises is repetition. You should repeat your breathing, repeat your mantra, and repeat your concentration on a single item. With visualization you can choose to return at a later session to the same sanctuary, or explore other locations every day. The repetitive nature of the exercise is selecting locales that allow you to experience harmony and peace ,and are unique and personalized for your circumstances.

Chapter 13: Meditation: Step By Step

Guide

By now, you are certainly aware that meditation offers tremendous positive benefits not only to the physical body, but entire well-being as well. You may have also decided to give it a shot, but you just don't know where to start.

The secret to engaging in an effective meditation practice is to choose the technique that will work for you. So, it will pay to try out several meditation types of tools to see which you will be most comfortable at.

If you are a bit clueless, try these "mindfulness meditation techniques:

Step 1: Choose a Location for Meditation

The meditation you should pick must be free from disruptions. Ideally, the spot must be comfortable, secured and peaceful. Your own bedroom is a favorable place to meditate or any corner in your house or other spots where you can spend a few minutes alone.

Once you have found a place, clean in it and remove the clutter. You may also surround the place with stuffs like candles, flowers and other accents that will add up to the tranquility of the place.

Step 2: Take a Comfortable Position

There are different positions to take, but you don't have to make things too hard by assuming complicated and uncomfortable positions. You can just sit in a chair or on your bed and that's it. These positions are easy and comfortable.

The important thing is to sit upright in order to promote energy flow. You may also use pillows and cushions, but make sure to remain upright. Lying down may be relaxing, but this may just make you sleepy instead of being in the awareness state.

Step 3: Clear the Mind

Before you start, it is vital that you clear the mind—loosen up, breathe slowly and deeply as possible. So, try taking a few slow and deep breaths by inhaling through the nose and breathing out to the mouth. Then, breathe at a regular or natural pace.

As a beginner, it will help if you focus on a thing or stimuli like music perhaps. Concentrating on a visual thing is a good way to occupy the mind and help it attain consciousness in a higher level. This is where you mediate with open eyes. As much as possible, choose objects like statues, candle flames and flowers among others. The object should be placed within eye level–stare at it until you feel the dimness and the thing fills your vision. What you will feel is deep calmness when there are no other stimuli than the object passes your brain.

Focusing on a mantra is also advisable. A mantra can be described as a single word or phrases that you chant or say to yourself repeatedly in a silent manner while meditating. This is to make you focus your attention to one thing than many thoughts.

You may try mantras like the "so hum" or other chants -this is ideal for beginners. The good thing with this is it is not in a language that you could easily associate things with. It is actually in Sanskrit that literally means "I am".

Later on, you may try clearing your mind without visual image or mantra.

Step 4: Observe

Stay in the position and simply let your inner dialogue drift. Observe you are feeling and thinking, but don't absorb.

You don't have to put yourself in anon-thinking mode". Instead, allow your mind to simply think without engaging in your thoughts. Watch your thoughts passively and let them be.

For instance, if you suddenly think: "I have work tomorrow" is just okay. But when you feel annoyed or think of the tasks you need to do, that means "engaging". That is a big "NO" in meditation. Your role in meditation is not to engage, but to simply observe such thoughts.

A great way of sensing when you have lost your focus is to do the counting. It is like counting from 1 to 10 repeatedly. When you notice that you are beyond the last number, simply go back to 1.

Do this for a few minutes or as long as you can. 2 to 3 minutes a day is good then, gradually lengthens your meditation time as you wish. The longer the time you allot for meditation, the deeper the consciousness you will develop.

Step 5: Ending Your Session

Once you are finish meditating, unhurriedly return to the physical reality in your surrounding and your body. Doing this may take a few seconds or a minute. When you meditate with your eyes closed, open your eyes slowly and adjust yourself to the surroundings. Abruptly opening your eyes can be trembling.

Remain in your position and reflect on certain feelings or thoughts and other things that ascended during your session. It is also a good practice to appreciate all the things to you feel thankful for in life.

Chapter 14: You Are Already

"Meditating"?

If you are a beginner then it's quite likely that you are trying to meditate for the very first time. But I bet you are not sure how, right? Well, it may be that you are already doing it in a way, but you are not aware of it. It took me a while also to become aware of it.

Read carefully, this may change the way you are looking at meditation and your life in general.

Think of something you like to do. Maybe you love to paint, maybe you love to walk your dog every day, maybe you like to dance, or maybe you keep journals.

Now, how do you feel while doing these things? Do you feel effortlessly happy and relaxed? Probably, because those are the things you love to do, and you are fully committed while doing them.

Let's say you love music and dancing. The feeling that you have when you're listening to loud music and maybe dancing like nobody's watching (thank God) is the most liberating feeling you could ever have, am I right?

There are situations when the body, through its movement, and the mind, through its lack of thinking, come into collision; and then a person starts to feel like she's been released from a prison and even may start to cry.

Especially when a person feels gratefulness and awareness at the same time.

This could happen to you also because all your emotions are coming out and you feel alive. That's the key to everything— YOU FEEL ALIVE. That's meditation, my dear reader.

Feel alive and be present. Be focused now. Be present now in this moment, in this life. You don't need to be sitting as a Buddha three times a day if that's not your thing. Maybe you like to write or paint, and sometimes hours can pass by and you

don't even notice. That's passion. That's
true beauty.

Chapter 15: The Meditation Process

You should never meditate directly after food as this is a time of day when your digestion can be disturbed. It is far better to meditate before the evening meal or in the mornings before breakfast. This helps you because these are peaceful times. You should make sure that you are in an area where you will not be disturbed and which is comfortable. I always make sure that the window is open so that there is fresh air, but don't do this if this causes a draught.

Get into position for meditation, but make sure that the clothing you wear is not in any way restrictive. Tight waistlines are not a good idea and if you feel more comfortable, take your shoes off. It is helpful to use a cushion if you are going to meditate on a mat because this helps you to place your legs in the right position as it lifts your behind from the floor. This is a lot easier for beginners.

Start with breathing exercises:

- Breathe in through the nostrils to the count of six
- Hold the air inside you for the count of five
- Breathe out to the count of eight.

When you are breathing correctly, you should notice that the upper abdomen pivots in and out and you need to keep breathing like this until you are comfortable with the rhythm of your breathing.

Starting the Meditation process

- Breathe in through the nostrils to the count of six
- Hold the air inside you for the count of five,
- Breathe out to the count of eight

While you are breathing, imagine the air as solid matter. You need to concentrate on the air coming into and leaving your body rather than letting your mind think of anything else at all. After each sequence as above you start to count from one to ten. For example, do the breathing exercise above and then count one. Do it again and then count two, etc. The idea is to reach ten without thinking of anything else at all.

What you will find is that thoughts come into your head regardless of you wanting them there. Again, as in the previous chapter, learn to dismiss the thoughts and imagine them as written out pieces of paper that you are going to let go into the wind. Do not attach any sentiment to the thoughts and do not let them form chains of thoughts. You have to learn to let go and dismiss these thoughts and then go back to your counting process by doing the breathing exercise and counting one again.

Each time a thought gets in the way, you go back to counting ONE and then onward to try and reach ten.

Are you likely to achieve this first time?

It is unlikely that you can do the breathing without thoughts getting into your mind. Your mind is accustomed to having thoughts and will find it quite hard at first to dismiss them and move on, but it needs to learn this. What you are doing is training the mind to focus upon what's important to your meditation process but this is also having an effect on the subconscious region as well and teaching it that you are in control. This will come in very useful when you want to achieve things in life or make yourself attractive to the right kinds of opportunities in your life using the laws of attraction.

Mind training is exceptionally useful in helping you to develop who you are and is particularly relevant to people who want to achieve their dreams in life instead of simply resenting the lives that they feel obligated to live.

Chapter 16: Color Imagination Healing

Meditation by Color Imagination healing

We as a human consist of a physical body, a fogging mind and internal spirit. The enormous energy within the components of these bodies converts from physical to spiritual energy. Whenever there is a blockage of flow between these energies, there arises a set of complications & Illnesses & sometimes this result in severe manifestations of certain un-ending scenarios. To heal these bad situations, there needs to be required the restoration of the broken path of these energies. Restoration also requires complete cleaning of negative energies which can be achieved through energies of color. Healing Meditation though color imagination and concentration works with miracles.

Procedures:

1. Take your Sitting position with comfort and close your eyes.

2. Imagine a strong visualize feeling, there is a large ring or ball of emanating golden colored light above your head. Imagine your inner insight is filling with golden light and the golden light is slowly descending through your head and crown area.

3. You will imagine that this golden light is nurturing your soul, cleaning your inner wounds and healing you completely and you will feel your spirit is free from toxic negative energies and you will feel lighter and energized.

4. Now change your imagination and feel ring or ball of Red light instead. Complete the process as done for the golden light. Complete the entire spectrum of light of Orange light, Yellow light, Green light, Blue light, Indigo light and Violet light. You can use your framed imagination as well for colors whichever you like at your own pace.

5. Hold the generated energy within your soul by keeping yourself in complete set of peace and calmness.

Chapter 17: Signs That a Person Is

Overloaded By Stress

A man that has stress over-burden can create physical side effects, for example, irritated stomach, cerebral pains, back and neck throbs or now and again chest tightening. Numerous individuals think that it's difficult to rest. Others encounter misery or even dejection.

A few people encounter tension or fits of anxiety. A man that encountering alarm assaults can endure indications that incorporate hustling heart, hyperventilation or breathing challenges, and also chest torment, queasiness or wooziness, cerebral pains, shaking and trembling, and significantly more.

Different manifestations of stress over-burden can be a sentiment being always constrained, bothered and on edge. A few people wind up peevish or testy.

Since stress can influence the resistant framework a few people encounter unfavorably susceptible responses, for example, skin inflammation or asthma. Stress can likewise make individuals more defenseless to colds and seasonal influenza.

A few people manage the manifestations of stress by drinking excessively, smoking, indulging, or taking medications. Despite the fact that these can briefly take out the side effects, the negative effects of these sorts of practices far exceed the advantages.

Monitor Stress

Since stress is unavoidable it is imperative to discover approaches to diminish and stay away from stressful responses to episodes in our lives. There are numerous strategies, from NLP and spellbinding methods to appropriate breathing, meditation, Tai Chi, knead, sound treatment and progressively that can enable you to balance the effects of stress.

Chapter 18: Reflection To Cause Rest

Resting supplements are intended to be made use of for a quick time duration to obtain your physical body back right into a rest pattern, however a great numerous Americans are utilizing them all of the time. Resting supplements are one of the most mistreated of all prescription medicines.

If you resemble many people, you have actually endured sometimes from insomnia. Sleep problems afflicts a lot of us at once or one more as well as has a selection of various sources. The majority of people decide to take medicine when sleeping disorders comes to be way too much of a concern to birth.

If you wish to reach rest normally, you could attempt reflection. Reflection to remove sleep problems is quite efficient and also is not unsafe like taking resting tablets. No one has actually ever before passed away from an overdose of reflection.

To efficient practice meditation to get over sleep problems, do the following:

1. Hinge on a comfy location on your bed. Make certain that you are entirely comfy as well as all set to head to rest.

Your very own individual paradise where every little thing is as you desire it. Begin with the environment of the best area and also start to assume of the kind of residence that you would certainly have in this location and also develop it in your mind.

3. After you have actually produced the location as well as home of your individual paradise, begin integrating just what kind of aroma would certainly welcome you at the doorway when you stroll right into your paradise. Would certainly it be a soft fragrance or the scent of something great food preparation in the stove?

4. Beginning integrating just what sort of home furnishings you would certainly have in this individual paradise. Down to the shade of the couch.

By managing your ideas prior to you go to rest, you could be able to regulate your rest state. Simply make certain that you see your very own individual paradise when you are going to rest and also not at job, driving or when you are expected to be doing something else.

Some may assert that this is simply fantasizing. Visiting your very own individual paradise is a kind of fantasizing, however with one distinction - you are not enabling your ideas to stray, you are regulating your ideas. Fantasizing is generally the outcome of obtaining burnt out at the office or college as well as enabling your ideas to roam to one more area.

Opportunities are, prior to you reach the kind of garments in your wardrobe in your individual paradise, you will certainly locate on your own asleep. You might also long for your very own individual paradise. Each evening, when you falling asleep, you could see your personal individual paradise.

Quickly, your physical body will certainly link your very own individual paradise ideas with rest and also you will certainly be able to go to rest when you see this fantastic area.

Believe regarding some conveniences you would certainly such as to have in your very own paradise. Believe concerning LCD tvs, Ipods or various other gizmos that you would certainly such as to possess.

Resting tablets are expected to be made use of for a quick time duration to obtain your physical body back right into a rest pattern, yet an excellent numerous Americans are utilizing them all of the time. Each evening, when you go to rest, you could see your very own individual paradise.

Simply make certain that you see your very own individual paradise when you are going to rest as well as not at job, driving or when you are meant to be doing something else. You desire to link this pleasurable location with going to rest.

Unlike various other reflection that you could do whenever you desire, insomnia reflection ought to just be utilized when you are prepared to go to rest. Quickly, your physical body will certainly link your very own individual paradise ideas with rest and also you will certainly be able to go to rest when you see this fantastic location.

By regulating your ideas prior to you go to rest, you could be able to manage your rest state. You will most likely fantasize regarding your individual paradise every now and then, however not all the moment. Various other points that went through your head and also made a perception on you throughout the day will certainly be blended in with yoru desires.

Offer on your own something to do in your individual paradise. Do you merely lounge about? Provide this duty to on your own.

Utilizing reflection to drop asleep is an old method. That is reflection. You get rid of various other ideas from your mind as well as permit the lamb take over.

Bring others right into the paradise. Make them component of your individual paradise.

Chapter 19: Meditation In Your Daily

Tasks

There are many things in our life that we find boring because they are part of our daily routine. We do them every day and we do them more or less the same way all the time. But you can make these daily routines more worthwhile if you integrate them as part of your mindfulness exercise. They are actually ideal for being part of your mediation routine since they are activities that you perform thoughtlessly and don't require creative thinking.

Chores

We all find chores boring to do, but some people have found the way to make chores more engaging is by doing them mindfully. This makes them more relaxing since it enables them to focus their attention on the process of doing these ordinary tasks.

The simplest way to perform mindfulness meditation while doing chores is simply to keep your focus on the physical act of doing them. To illustrate how this works, let's say you're doing the dishes. Start by taking a deep breath to center yourself. Then start doing the washing. Make sure that your mind is focused on the way your hands are washing the dishes. For example, focus on the movement of your hands as they lather the dishes with soap, rinse them and then dry them.

Of course, you will probably notice that your mind tends to wander while doing your chores. When this happens you should pause and gently put your mind back on what you're doing. This may be difficult since you probably don't like what you're doing but you should be patient and avoid resistance.

Eating and Drinking

Eating is another regular task that we tend to do mindlessly and without too much thought. Unless you're eating something you particularly like, you probably eat food simply by shoveling it into your mouth without consideration as to how it tastes. In fact, many people no longer take pleasure in the daily process of eating, since they think of it as something that they have to do so that they can go on to do something that they would rather do, such as play video games or engage in other fun activities. But eating mindfully will hopefully teach you how to appreciate the daily process of eating food again.

Start by taking a couple of deep breaths when you sit at the table to eat. Then focus on the physical sensations you experience when you're eating. For example, when you put the food into your mouth, what does it taste like? What does it feel like on your tongue? Is it hot or cold? Also, think about what you're eating. What is it? What are the different ingredients that you taste? If you're eating with your hands, what is the texture of the food on your fingers? Is it smooth? Does it feel grainy? Does it feel warm?

In addition, you should focus on what you're feeling while you're eating. Do you feel engaged in the activity? Do you feel impatient? Are you in a hurry to finish? What do you feel about the food you're eating? Do you like it? Do you have a problem with certain aspects of the taste? Do you find it too salty or sweet? Make sure that you chew your food thoroughly while you're eating.

Take a moment to appreciate the food that you're eating. Even if you don't like it, you should be thankful that it is there for you to have. Finally, once you're finished eating, take a moment to reflect on it. What is the aftertaste of the food in your mouth? Did you enjoy what you've just eaten?

Another thing that you can notice is how your feelings change while you're eating.

You may notice that you're very hungry when you start and then those feelings gradually abate as you get fuller. Simply keep noting your feelings without judging them.

You can also follow the same process when you're enjoying a cup of coffee or other beverage. When you hold the cup, what does it feel like in your hands? Is it hot or cold? When you bring it to your mouth, what does it smell like? Try inhaling more deeply so that the smell more deeply enters your nose.

As with any other meditation, you should expect your mind to start wandering while you're doing it. You can avoid this problem by starting with just doing this exercise for just a minute or two and then gradually moving up, first to five minutes and then eventually to fifteen. What is important is that you stay in the moment while you're eating.

Chapter 20: Forgiveness

Like equanimity, learning to forgive means confronting the damage not forgiving does to us on the inside. Anger, resentment, jealousy, blame, and other negative emotions, are like a second hit we do to ourselves after receiving the first external blow. As with equanimity, when you are just beginning to meditate, it is best to start with a small issue so that you are not overwhelmed by your feelings. As you practice and get more powerful in your meditations, you can tackle bigger and bigger issues.

Forgiveness does not mean we excuse a behavior. Forgiveness means we make amends externally as we should—but also that we do not allow the negative emotions associated with what we have done to haunt our minds. Ask yourself: if a very close friend had done what you have done, how would you counsel them? Would you suggest they stay haunted by what they had done for the rest of their lives—as we often do to ourselves? Of course not. You would tell them to make up for what they had done if they could, to accept inside that they made a mistake, and to promise themselves to do better in the future.

On the other hand, sometimes we feel other people have wronged us. It could be something simple, like being cut off in traffic. You grit your teeth and grip the wheel, and allow this anger to tear through the rest of your evening like an angry bull after a red cape. You are distracted during dinner, perhaps are not as attentive to your family as you should be, and grit your teeth while you try to watch some TV. Meanwhile, the person who cut you off has arrived home and is enjoying a relaxing evening, not having given the same situation that is troubling you a second thought.

Begin your forgiveness meditation as you do your equanimity meditation, but focusing on your posture, breath, and muscles until you are in a meditative state. Now, carefully move your attention from your breath to these thoughts:

I forgive myself...

For making mistakes, for not understanding, for hurting myself and others.

Keep focused on these thoughts. If you feel overwhelmed by negative emotions, temporarily return to focusing on your breathing until you once again feel centered in a meditative state. Then slowly return to these thoughts. If it feels too much for now, then simply focus on your breathing and end your meditation. Return to this issue in the future when you feel ready.

Now, center yourself on your breathing once again. When you are ready, move your attention to these thoughts:

I forgive you...
For not understanding, for making mistakes, for hurting me and others.

As with forgiving yourself, this practice can dredge up powerful emotions. If they become too strong, simply focus again on your breathing, acknowledging the emotions and allowing them to fade away as you focus on your breath. Return to the thoughts if you feel able, or end your meditation and return to them in the future.

Chapter 21: How To Skyrocket Your

Creativity With Meditation

In a previous chapter, I made an introduction on how meditation could help you get new ideas and feel more motivated and in this chapter I will be focused on showing you exact steps with all the benefits that meditation will bring and how it affects creativity levels.

Focus- It is the key in resolving every problem. Meditation can be a powerful tool that you can use to brainstorm solutions to any problem or a specific problem. Key is to focus on listing solutions. Meditation will calm your mind as well as get your system used to becoming more creative. Ultimately, all creativity is an act of channeling source. Solutions can come to you in the form of ideas or synchronicities. Your job is really to spend some time in meditation and let go. You may receive ideas instantly or later. You may accidentally meet a coworker a week later who tells you about a resource that eventually solves your problem.

Patience- You need to be patient when it comes to meditation. You cannot expect huge results immediately and your creativity won't be skyrocketed after three days. You need constant and regular meditation if you want your creativity levels to go higher! Ultimately this is not an endeavor to grow your creativity constantly to higher and higher levels. Rather this is a practice that easily allows you to get into a creative mode.

Calmness- I was terrified the first time I start meditating because I realized how much my mind was occupied with unimportant stuff, problems of other people, and opinions of personas I do not really care about. Just keep calm once when you realize how busy your mind is.

Perspective- Once you try meditation, you will realize how many problems and worries you have today that are not important at all. You will see a bigger picture. You will realize that nothing is as important as saving your body from getting more stressed. Also you can explore in your mind multiple perspectives of the same situation.

Learn the steps of basic meditation and where to start

When people find out about meditation, they usually ask themselves the same question: "Where and how to start and what will be the method that will help me the most?"

The best thing, which I recommend to beginners and novices in meditation and meditation process, is to start with the basics. Just sit, put your legs in front of you (you can cross them if you want), close your eyes and simply focus just on breathing. Nothing else!

Once when you realize how easy it is, you can move onto other methods of meditation. You can also explore movement meditation as well as walking meditation. Some of them might work better for you.

How long a session should last?

This is a great question. Many people find it difficult to sit for 15-20 minutes and think about nothing. I understand and that is why I recommend you to start with only 5 minutes! 5- minute sessions do not look so bad, right? I think you can do it! And later when you are ready, you can scale up.

Another thing you need to do once when you start meditating is to turn off all the distractions. You do not need your TV turned on and loud music in the background. You also need to turn off your mobile phone because you do not want to be interrupted during your session. A good thing to do would be to set up an alarm so you do not feel the need to constantly look at your clock and see whether your session is done.

Chapter 22: Using Meditation For Goals

Meditation helps you get to know yourself and gain access to deeper parts of your mind where you may have never had access. This means that meditation allows you to give yourself direct messages. If you want to change something about yourself or end a bad habit, you can use meditation to tell your subconscious to stop this habit. Your subconscious will listen in the meditative state because it is more impressionable in the theta state. In addition, the soothing relief that you get from meditation helps you stop certain habits that are born from stress, such as smoking or emotional overeating. You can heal yourself and watch many of your flaws and bad habits flake away.

This does not mean that meditation is a quick and easy solution to everything that you hate about yourself. Meditation takes time and work. So don't be disappointed if you don't lose twenty pounds or suddenly feel no desire to drink alcohol after you meditate once. You have to invest the effort to healing and improving yourself.

You also need to drop the attitude that you are inherently flawed and you need to conform to social standards of perfection. If you hold this attitude, you are going against the gentle attitude of acceptance and self-love that meditation brings. Meditation can help chip away at this attitude and help you come to love yourself as you are. But you should try to start thinking this way anyway, and you should start to treat yourself with love and acceptance. Don't view meditation as some easy escape from all that you hate about yourself, or you will unintentionally stress yourself out and defeat the whole purpose of meditation, which is to clear your mind of distressing clutter, heal your heart, and relieve yourself of stress.

Meditation will make you want to live a better and cleaner lifestyle. As you get in touch with yourself, you will hear your body and mind scream for better self-care. You realize what you secretly want and need, which is always healthy. The bad habits that you currently hold will no longer seem appealing to you. However, you should help this process along by improving your lifestyle from the start. A good lifestyle is a great companion to meditation and it will help you feel better instantly. It will increase your self-esteem, enabling you to become the person that you want to be.

Stress can also be relieved by exercise. Exercise can teach you the mental endurance that you need to become adept at meditation. Consider it training to become a mental ninja and a master of your own self. How cool is that? It certainly feels great. I recommend yoga or Tai Chi to help you learn this self-control while also relieving stress and improving your health.

Diet is also important. If you consume a lot of sugar, alcohol, or caffeine, you naturally increase your stress. Processed carbs and food dyes are also best to avoid as much as you can. The more healthy foods that you put into your body, the better you will feel. Say good-bye to brain fog, depression, anxiety, stress, and other physical and mental issues all at once. This will aid you in the self-improvement that you aim to achieve with meditation.

Meditation and a healthy lifestyle work hand-in-hand. Meditation encourages you to live a healthier life, while a healthy lifestyle helps you achieve results from meditation more quickly. You can really fix yourself and improve who you are as a person with these two elements.

How to Perform Meditation for Self-Improvement

While I cover specific examples and meditations after this, I will go over some of the main steps that you must keep in mind when using meditation to achieve some sort of self-improvement goal.

First, you want to set a clear goal for yourself. Write this goal down to cement it into your brain. For some reason, writing things down help your brain remember them better. Now, with your goal on a piece of paper in front of you, tell yourself that this is your goal for your meditation today. Repeat this goal three times to really emphasize it. This draws the attention of your subconscious if you repeat the goal, as it tells your brain that you are serious about what you are saying and that something is vital.

Guide your meditation around this goal. Think about achieving it. Visualize achieving it. Then, envision what it looks like once you achieve this goal. Say you want to lose weight. How do you look skinny? How do you feel? How do other people see you now? How will your life change, and what benefits will arise? Focus on this for a while.

After this, go about your meditation. Work on clearing your mind and relaxing your body. Slip into your meditative state. Enjoy this time with yourself and don't worry about your goal. When you have basked in this calm for a while, you can enter a guided imagery scenario, where you work on addressing your goal. You can envision how your life looks without your bad habit, or you can practice skills that you would like to develop to deal with your habit in real life.

When you finally bring yourself back to full consciousness, think about your goal once again. Envision it again. Envision what the future will look like, with your goal completed.

This part may seem silly, but it is actually the most crucial part of this entire meditative process. Shower yourself with pride and self-love. Really let yourself feel proud of yourself. Give yourself a pat on the back and congratulate yourself. You have just started the journey toward your goal, and you will complete it. That deserves a celebration. Don't be bashful about congratulating yourself, no matter how awkward it feels. We are so used to being hard on ourselves that being nice to ourselves often feels weird. But it is actually a good thing to show yourself some love now and then. It won't go to your head and make you an egotistical jerk, so don't even worry about that. It will simply make you feel stronger and it will bring more peace into your life as you quiet the hateful chatter in your mind that you criticize yourself with.

Now let's explore a few great meditations that can help you get to the core of your problems and end bad habits. These meditations are specifically designed for self-improvement goals.

Quitting Smoking

If you smoke, you probably already want to quit for many reasons. I don't need to tell you why quitting smoking is important. However, you may have a lot of trouble ending this habit. Nicotine addiction is hard to break, but not impossible. Meditation can really help in this case.

The best thing to do is to repeat an affirmation about how you want to quit smoking as you enter your meditation. Once you reach the theta state, start envisioning how your life will be when you quit. Imagine how clean you will smell, how much extra cash you will have in your wallet, and how clear your lungs will feel. Picture going to the doctor and getting a clean bill of health. If you have asthma, imagine a day without wheezing and coughing because you are no longer taxing your lungs with smoke. When you bring yourself out of this meditation again, repeat your affirmations.

It may take you a few weeks to see results. But the more you perform this meditation, the less you will want to smoke.

Quitting Worrying

Meditation alone will help you overcome the habit of worrying. But practicing mindfulness meditation is particularly helpful in this case. Really work on grounding your mind for a while on the present exclusively. Learn to pull your mind to the present when you start to become obsessed with worries and concerns. Your mind doesn't need to be wandering and stopping on hypothetical situations that may never come to pass. It only needs to be concerned with the present. Now, get into the habit of pulling your mind into the present using mindfulness meditation tricks whenever you start to worry, even when you are not in meditation. Apply mindfulness to your everyday life until it becomes a habit and a way of life for you.

Stop Overeating

Gluttony is a very harmful activity that can really bust your self-esteem and make you gain weight. To stop overeating, you need to identify what causes you to stuff your face. Most likely, you overeat to compensate for some sense of emptiness or lack within your heart. Now, in meditation, ask your subconscious to fill this hole with gold. Even imagine a great pit within you being filled.

Another cause of overeating is that you are trying to soothe away symptoms of stress. It is best to work on stress relief. Then, your overeating problem will probably resolve itself.

If you continue to have this habit even when you are able to release stress from your mind, then try to practice constraint through meditation exercises. In meditation, imagine heaps of food in front of you. But imagine that you are not allowed to touch this food or you will suffer disastrous consequences, in the form of some sort of punishment. Practice walking by the food in your meditation without touching a morsel. Then, work on eating only a little bit and abstaining from overeating. Teach your mind the art of moderation through meditation.

End Cravings

When your cravings for bad things, such as drugs, cigarettes, alcohol, bad food, or gambling, become sharp, it is essential to push them away. Don't repress them or they will never go away. Instead, acknowledge that you are craving. Let yourself feel the sharpness of the craving for a moment. Then dismiss it and go about your day. Draw your thoughts away from the hypothetical situation where you satisfy your craving and instead focus on whatever you are doing at the time, like washing dishes, driving, or working.

If you can, take the time that you feel cravings the worst to enter meditation. Spend your meditation focusing on feeling things other than the instant gratification that you receive from satisfying whatever craving you have.

Think More Positively

Positive thinking is a habit that meditation can help you develop. While you meditate, tell your subconscious to think more positively. Identify your negative thoughts. Even view them as people or objects, lined up in a row, while you are deep in meditation. Now disable or transform each of these people or objects into a more positive image that brings you greater joy. For instance, if your mother was abusive and now you think a lot of negative things about yourself thanks to her constant criticism, you may want to picture your mother in your meditation. Tell her that you don't appreciate the mean messages that she gives you, and then turn her image into a happier one. Try to attribute more positive memories to her and try to imagine her sharp words coming out as gentle, kind ones.

The mental control you gain during meditation can help you ward off negative thinking even when you aren't meditating. Let these negative thoughts move through your mind, unobstructed. Allow yourself to hear them and feel the pain that they cause. Then, let them go. Replace them with more positive thoughts and really feel the joy or happiness that these thoughts bring you. Work on this often until you think more positive thoughts than negative ones.

About The Author

Jay Lucado is born wth the vision to promote
the art of meditation among the masses. The
author has written several research papers on
the topic. He has served as an instructor
promoting various cultural arts in University of
San Francisco. He is currently living with his
wife in California.

CPSIA information can be obtained
at www.ICGtesting.com
Printed in the USA
BVHW092245080922
646639BV00008B/101

9 781999 297909